# The history of imbanking and draining the fens and marshes, and of the improvements intended thereby; extracted from records, manuscripts, and other authentic testimonies.

## William Dugdale

*The history of imbanking and draining the fens and marshes, and of the improvements intended thereby; extracted from records, manuscripts, and other authentic testimonies. By Sir William Dugdale, ... A new edition, revised and corrected from the edition of 1662. With several additions; illustrated with a new set of maps. By the Rev. George William Lemon, ...*

Dugdale, William, Sir

ESTCID: T167572

Reproduction from Cambridge University Library

First published in 1662 as 'The history of imbanking and drayning of divers fenns and marshes'.

Lynn : printed by W. Whittingham, and sold by S. Crowder, London, 1792.

[4],ii,[2],34p.,plates : maps ; 4°

## Gale ECCO Print Editions

Relive history with *Eighteenth Century Collections Online*, now available in print for the independent historian and collector. This series includes the most significant English-language and foreign-language works printed in Great Britain during the eighteenth century, and is organized in seven different subject areas including literature and language; medicine, science, and technology; and religion and philosophy. The collection also includes thousands of important works from the Americas.

The eighteenth century has been called "The Age of Enlightenment." It was a period of rapid advance in print culture and publishing, in world exploration, and in the rapid growth of science and technology – all of which had a profound impact on the political and cultural landscape. At the end of the century the American Revolution, French Revolution and Industrial Revolution,  perhaps three of the most significant events in modern history, set in motion developments that eventually dominated world political, economic, and social life.

In a groundbreaking effort, Gale initiated a revolution of its own: digitization of epic proportions to preserve these invaluable works in the largest online archive of its kind. Contributions from major world libraries constitute over 175,000 original printed works. Scanned images of the actual pages, rather than transcriptions, recreate the works *as they first appeared.*

Now for the first time, these high-quality digital scans of original works are available via print-on-demand, making them readily accessible to libraries, students, independent scholars, and readers of all ages.

For our initial release we have created seven robust collections to form one the world's most comprehensive catalogs of 18th century works.

*Initial Gale ECCO Print Editions collections include:*

### History and Geography

Rich in titles on English life and social history, this collection spans the world as it was known to eighteenth-century historians and explorers. Titles include a wealth of travel accounts and diaries, histories of nations from throughout the world, and maps and charts of a world that was still being discovered. Students of the War of American Independence will find fascinating accounts from the British side of conflict.

*Social Science*

Delve into what it was like to live during the eighteenth century by reading the first-hand accounts of everyday people, including city dwellers and farmers, businessmen and bankers, artisans and merchants, artists and their patrons, politicians and their constituents. Original texts make the American, French, and Industrial revolutions vividly contemporary.

*Medicine, Science and Technology*

Medical theory and practice of the 1700s developed rapidly, as is evidenced by the extensive collection, which includes descriptions of diseases, their conditions, and treatments. Books on science and technology, agriculture, military technology, natural philosophy, even cookbooks, are all contained here.

*Literature and Language*

Western literary study flows out of eighteenth-century works by Alexander Pope, Daniel Defoe, Henry Fielding, Frances Burney, Denis Diderot, Johann Gottfried Herder, Johann Wolfgang von Goethe, and others. Experience the birth of the modern novel, or compare the development of language using dictionaries and grammar discourses.

*Religion and Philosophy*

The Age of Enlightenment profoundly enriched religious and philosophical understanding and continues to influence present-day thinking. Works collected here include masterpieces by David Hume, Immanuel Kant, and Jean-Jacques Rousseau, as well as religious sermons and moral debates on the issues of the day, such as the slave trade. The Age of Reason saw conflict between Protestantism and Catholicism transformed into one between faith and logic -- a debate that continues in the twenty-first century.

*Law and Reference*

This collection reveals the history of English common law and Empire law in a vastly changing world of British expansion. Dominating the legal field is the *Commentaries of the Law of England* by Sir William Blackstone, which first appeared in 1765. Reference works such as almanacs and catalogues continue to educate us by revealing the day-to-day workings of society.

*Fine Arts*

The eighteenth-century fascination with Greek and Roman antiquity followed the systematic excavation of the ruins at Pompeii and Herculaneum in southern Italy; and after 1750 a neoclassical style dominated all artistic fields. The titles here trace developments in mostly English-language works on painting, sculpture, architecture, music, theater, and other disciplines. Instructional works on musical instruments, catalogs of art objects, comic operas, and more are also included.

**The BiblioLife Network**

This project was made possible in part by the BiblioLife Network (BLN), a project aimed at addressing some of the huge challenges facing book preservationists around the world. The BLN includes libraries, library networks, archives, subject matter experts, online communities and library service providers. We believe every book ever published should be available as a high-quality print reproduction; printed on-demand anywhere in the world. This insures the ongoing accessibility of the content and helps generate sustainable revenue for the libraries and organizations that work to preserve these important materials.

The following book is in the "public domain" and represents an authentic reproduction of the text as printed by the original publisher. While we have attempted to accurately maintain the integrity of the original work, there are sometimes problems with the original work or the micro-film from which the books were digitized. This can result in minor errors in reproduction. Possible imperfections include missing and blurred pages, poor pictures, markings and other reproduction issues beyond our control. Because this work is culturally important, we have made it available as part of our commitment to protecting, preserving, and promoting the world's literature.

**GUIDE TO FOLD-OUTS MAPS and OVERSIZED IMAGES**

The book you are reading was digitized from microfilm captured over the past thirty to forty years. Years after the creation of the original microfilm, the book was converted to digital files and made available in an online database.

In an online database, page images do not need to conform to the size restrictions found in a printed book. When converting these images back into a printed bound book, the page sizes are standardized in ways that maintain the detail of the original. For large images, such as fold-out maps, the original page image is split into two or more pages

Guidelines used to determine how to split the page image follows:

• Some images are split vertically; large images require vertical and horizontal splits.
• For horizontal splits, the content is split left to right.
• For vertical splits, the content is split from top to bottom.
• For both vertical and horizontal splits, the image is processed from top left to bottom right.

A MAP of the great LEVEL of the FENS, together with the Rivers that pass thro' the said LEVEL into the BAY, call'd METARIS ÆSTUARIUM.

NORTHAMPTONSHIRE

LINCOLN SHIRE

HUNTINGTONSHIRE

CAMBRIDGE SHIRE

SUFFOLK

NORFOLK

Holland

Bedford Level

Marshland

Holland Fen

Peterburgh

Stamford

Boston

KINGS LYN

Ely

Whittlesey Meere

Ramsey Meere

Spalding

Crowland

Deeping Fen

Wisbech

Upwell

Outwell

Denver

Downham

Stow

Jockey Bridge

Lyn Deeps

A Scale of Miles
5    10    15    20

# THE
# HISTORY
OF
# IMBANKING and DRAINING
THE
# FENS and MARSHES,

And of the IMPROVEMENTS intended thereby;

EXTRACTED FROM

RECORDS, MANUSCRIPTS, and other AUTHENTIC TESTIMONIES.

By Sir WILLIAM DUGDALE, Knt. GARTER Principal King at Arms.

A New EDITION, Revised and Corrected from the Edition of 1662. With several
ADDITIONS, Illustrated with a New Set of MAPS

> - - - - - - - - - - - - - - - - Quique Paludis
> Collectum humorem bibula deducit arenâ,
> Præter m incertis si mensibus annis abundans
> Exit, et obducto late tenet omnia limo,
> Unde cavæ tepido sudant humore lacunæ.
>
> GEO I v 113.

By the Rev. GEORGE WILLIAM LEMON,
Author of the ENGLISH DERIVATIVE DICTIONARY,
And the HISTORY of the CIVIL WARS between YORK and LANCASTER

LYNN;

Printed by W. WHITTINGHAM, and Sold by S. CROWDER,
Pater Noster Row, LONDON

MDCCXCII.

22 — 487

# THE
# AUTHOR's
## DEDICATION
### TO
# KING CHARLES II.

Moſt Gracious Sovereign,

THE firſt and greateſt attempt, that hath been made in this kingdom, for the general Drainage of thoſe vaſt Fens, lying in Cambridgeſhire, and the Counties adjacent, was by that prudent and grave prelate John Morton, ſometime Biſhop of Ely, as the Channel betwixt Peterborough and Wiſbeach, ſtill bearing his name, doth witneſs: And the next by your Royal Grand-father and Father; Which not ſucceeding, as it was deſigned, by reaſon of the diſtractions of thoſe times; it will be no ſmall Honour to your Sacred Majeſty, and Advantage of your Realm, to compleat and make perfect that Noble undertaking: To which end, I humbly offer unto your Majeſty this preſent Hiſtorical Diſcourſe; whereby it will appear, not only, that many Great and Mighty
Princes,

Princes, and other Perfons, famous in their times, have in Foreign parts been active in Works of this kind: but how much your Majefty's own Royal Anceftors have by feveral excellent and wholfome Laws promoted the like in this kingdom: Praying to the Almighty, that he will blefs your Majefty with a long and profperous Reign, that good Arts may again flourifh amongft us, and Virtue receive its due Encouragement, to the joy of all your Loyal Subjects; and amongft them, of

Your Majefty's

Moft obedient Subject,

and Faithful Servant,

WILLIAM DUGDALL.

TO

# TO THE

# READER,

*Courteous Reader,*

THAT the ſtrength of a king is in the multitude of his ſubjeƈts, is a truth which no man will gain-ſay. Hence it is, that thoſe Countries, the ſoil of which is naturally fruitfull, are always much better eſteem'd, than ſuch as are ſteril, in regard they afford more and better ſuſtenance to their inhabitants. And hence it is likewiſe that the moſt civilized Nations have by ſo much art and induſtry, endeavoured to make the beſt improvement of their Waſtes, Commons, and all ſorts of barren Land, amongſt which advantages, that of incloſure has not been the leaſt, of which there is a ſtriking inſtance in the Counties of Northampton, and Somerſet, which, though little differing in their extent and goodneſs of ſoil, yet, if eſtimation may be made, by Muſters, Subſidies, Tenths, and Fiſteenths, incloſure has made the one more than double to exceed the other, both in people, and wealth, as hath long ago been obſerved * by ſome of great Judgement

If then the mere incloſure and tillage of which naturally yielded little profit, does juſtly deſerve ſo great a commendation, how much more is the ſkill and pains of thoſe to be had in eſteem, who have recovered many vaſt proportions of Land, totally overwhelmed with a deluge of waters? And of theſe I need not look out for examples from abroad our own Country affording a multitude of notable inſtances, as the enſuing Diſcourſe will fully manifeſt, whereby it will appear, that in numerous parts of this Realm, there are many thouſands of Acres, which do now yield much benefit yearly, by Rye, Cole-ſeed, Graſs, Hay, Hemp, Flax, Wheat, Oats, and other Grain, nay by all ſorts of excellent Plants, Garden-ſtuff, and fruit Trees, which in former times were Drowned Lands.

And this it was, which gave encouragement to our two late Sovereigns of Bleſſed Memory, ( viz King James and King Charles the firſt ) to become the ſole Adventurers for the Draining of thoſe vaſt Fens of Cambridgeſhire, and the five adjacent Counties, ( a worthy Work, and never totally attempted till their times, ) well diſcerning, that by a compleat performance thereof, the coſtly and troubleſome meeting of commiſſioners for Sewers, the frequent great taxes, for the maintenance of divers Banks and Drains, with many unhappy controverſies and emulations relating to them, might be, in a great meaſure prevented And if our induſtry were but comparable to that of our neighbours in the Belgic Provinces, how much more might theſe drained grounds afford us, for profit and pleaſure, than they yet do? for as much as theirs, lying below the Level of the Sea at high tides, is drained by Engines, which caſt out the water, and ours have not only a deſcent to the Sea, but many large Rivers and ſtreams, for leading the waters to their natural out falls.

To give an inſtance in the benefits. Firſt let us conſider the large proportion of this one Level, which is no leſs than five hundred thouſand Acres, it being, from the edge of Suffolk, to Wayeſlete in Lincolnſhire, full Lxviii. miles in a ſtrait line :

* See the life of K. Edward vi. by Sir John Hayward, p 45

# TO THE READER.

'line: And if we reckon by the low of the Fen, which runs up both fides of the River Witham, within a mile of Lincoln, it may be well accounted Lxxx miles, the breadth being in many places xxx. more xx. and feldom fo little as ten miles: fo that, 'tis thought by fome, to be as good ground, and as much, as the States of the Low Countries enjoy in the Netherlands.

Next; for the richnefs of the Soil, being gained from the waters, does it not for the moft part exc ed the high grounds thereon bordering. as much as other meadows do, which are ordinarily let for xxs. the Acre? And do we not fee, that in Marfhes beyond Wayeflete in Lincolnfhire, where the grounds are fevered and trenched, it is hard to find a poor man, though they are fet at great Rents? for the cattle being always found and thriving, are therefore merchantable; or if they come to a mifchance, yet are fit for food.

Moreover; befides the great plenty of flefh and white meats, with breed of feveral horfes, let us confider the abundance of Wool, Hides, Tallow, and other articles, which this fruitful ground now produces; and that the new channels made for Draining, do yield no fmall advantage to all thofe parts, for the carriage of their Corn and Merchandize, whereas before, they were conftrained to go many miles about, according to the natural bending of the Rivers.

And if we weigh the great inconveniences, which thefe over-flowings have produced, certainly the advantage by the general Draining ought the more to be prized; for in Winter time, when the Ice is ftrong enough to hinder the paffage of Boats (as fome have well obferved) and yet not able to bear a man, the inhabitants upon the Hards, and the Banks within the Fens, can have no help of food, nor comfort for body or foul, no woman aided in her travail, no means to baptize a child, or partake of the communion, nor fupply of any neceffary, except what thofe poor defolate places may afford. And what expectation of health can there be to the bodies of men, where there is no element good? the Air being for the moft part cloudy, grofs, and full of rotten harrs. the Water putrid and muddy, yea full of loathfome infects, the Earth fpungy and boggy, and the Fire noifome by the ftink of fmokey Haffocks.

As for the decay of Fifh and Fowl, which hath been no fmall objection againft this public work, there is not much likelihood thereof. for notwithftanding this general Draining, there are fo many great Meeres and Lakes, ftill continuing. which are indeed the principal harbours for them, that there will be no want of either; for in the vaft fpreading waters they feldom abide, the Rivers, Channels, and Meeres being their chief Receptacles; which being now increafed, will rather augment, than diminifh their ftore And that both Fifh and Fowl are with much more eafe taken by this reftraint of the waters within fuch bounds, we daily fee; forafmuch as all Nets for Fifhing, are better made ufe of in the Rivers and Meeres, than when the waters are out of thofe narrower limits. And that Decoys are now planned upon many drained Levels, whereby greater numbers of Fowl are caught, than by any other Engines, formerly ufed; which could not at all be made there, did the waters, as ufual, overfpread the whole Country.

# THE
# HISTORY
## OF
# IMBANKING and DRAINING.

## CHAP. I.

THAT works of draining are moſt antient, and of divine inſtitution, we have the teſtimony of holy Scripture, § " In the beginning God ſaid, " Let the waters be gathered together, and let " the dry land appear, and it was ſo: † And " the earth brought forth graſs, and herb " yielding ſeed, and the fruit tree yielding " fruit after his kind, and God ſaw that it " was good.

Again, after the deluge, it was through the divine goodneſs, that * " the waters were dryed " up from off the earth, and the face of the " ground was dry.

And that thoſe nations, which are of great antiquity, and in chief renown for arts and civility, are alſo famous for their works of this nature, is evident from the practice of the *Egyptians*, the *Bayblonians*, the *Græcians*, the *Romans*, and ſeveral others, of which I ſhall give inſtances.

### EGYPT

Firſt therefore of EGYPT, ¶ " becauſe that " country is more marvelous than any other; " and that the works there, are more remark- " able than the country   This lyeth in a great length from ſouth to north, between ARABIA and LYBIA, and is watered with the river NILE· a ſtream that ‡ " all the Winter keeps within " its banks, but at the Summer ſolſtice be- " gins to exceed, and ſwelling an hundred " days, is almoſt as long a time in retreating. Which conſtant inundation is ſo commodious, that " thoſe ſurrounded parts, (as an eminent " hiſtorian § teſtifies) are only habitable; and " that whatſoever place on either ſide the ri- " ver, riſes in ſuch a manner, that it cannot " receive the flood, remains deſert and unin- " habited, through want of water.

We may therefore eſteem the *Egyptians* to have been the firſt maſters in this art of drain- ing, whom neceſſity and profit induced to im- ploy their wit and labour, to the improvement of their country, and making the beſt advan- tage of that extraordinary river · wherein they became moſt excellent, " their workmanſhip " about the river Nile, being ſuch (as the " ſame learned author obſerves) ‖ " that in- " duſtry ſurpaſſed nature   for Egypt (ſays " he) though naturally fruitful, being watered, " is more fruitful· and though, according to " the courſe of nature, the greateſt increaſe " of the river, overflows the moſt land, yet, " through induſtry, it was ſo brought to paſs, " that often, when nature was defective, there " was by the help of trenches and banks as " much ground watered with the ſmaller floods, " as with the greater   ſo that at high flood, " the country is all a ſea, except the cities and " villages, which, being ſituate, either on " natural hills, or artificial banks, at a diſtance " ſeem to be iſlands.

The

§ Gen 1 v 9 † Ver. 12 * Gen viii 13 ¶ Herod lib. ii. c. 35. ‡ idem. l ii. c. 19 § Strab. lib. xvii. p 786. ‖ idem p 787

" The juſt increaſe ‖ (of this flowing) appears
" to be xvi cubits leſs water would not be ſuf-
" ficient for all, more would be too flow in
" retreating; too much water keeping the
" ground wet too long, loſes the ſeaſon of
" ſowing too little affords no ſeaſon,
" through drought The country reckon up
" on both At xvi cubits they foreſee fa
" mine; at xiii, hunger, xiv bring mirth,
" xv, ſecurity, and xvi, plenty.

The Egyptian trenches therefore were of
two ſorts, either for carrying off ſuperfluous
water, or diſpoſing of what might be uſeful
there being evident examples of both kinds
Of the firſt ſort are thoſe many outlets made
by hand, for the river's freer paſſage to the
Mediterranean, the natural mouths of the
Nile being inſufficient for the *ſeptem oſtia*
were not all natural " § The Nile having run
" through Egypt in one ſtream, to the city of
" Cercaſorum, there divides itſelf into three
" channels, one runs eaſtward, towards Pe-
" luſium, the other weſtward, towards Cano-
" pus, from whence they are denominated, and
" the third, dividing Delta, runs ſtraight forward
" to Sebennytus, from whence its name, and
" there it is divided into two other ſtreams, the
" one paſſing by Sais, the other by Mendes,
" receive their names from thoſe cities: But the
" Bolbitique and Bucolique channels are not
" natural, but made by art

This iſland of Egypt towards the ſea, be
tween the Peluſiaque and Canobique channels,
is called Delta, " from the form of the letter
" inverted ſo ▽ " † Between theſe two mouths,
beſides the five before mentioned, " theſe are
" many ſmaller For from the former, there
" are divers ſubdiviſions, throughout the whole
" iſland, which make ſeveral water-courſes, and
" iſlands, ſo that one channel being cut into
" another, it is navigable every way " The rea
ſon why theſe lower parts were cut and drained
in ſuch an extraordinary manner, may be (beſides the convenience of navigation, for that they
were more apt to ſilting, of which the Egyptian
prieſts had great ſcience, For " in the reign
" of king Myris, when the river roſe not above
" eight cubits, it watered all Egypt below
" Memphis: But now " (in the time of Hero-
" dotus) ‡ unleſs it roſe xvi or at leaſt xv cubits,

" it overflowed not that part of the country
" nor was there nine hundred years paſſed from
" the death of king Myris, to the time that
" Herodotus heard this from the prieſts "

Amongſt this ſort of works againſt the inconveniences of the river, may be reckoned the
" imbanking ‡ of cities, which Seſoſtris firſt
" performed but thoſe works, eſpecially at
" Bubaſtis, were after heightened by Sabacon
" the Æthiopian, who employed therein all
" perſons condemned to death " The other
kind of trenches, extending the benefit of the
inundation beyond nature, is more commendable, having leſs of neceſſity, but more for
imitation The firſt or theſe was made by
king Mœris, into a lake on the Libyan ſide,
which bears his name " which lake " † ſays
Herodotus " is three thouſand and ſix hundred
" furlongs in compaſs (being the meaſure of
" Egypt along the ſea coaſt) and lies in length
" north and ſouth. the greateſt depth being
" fifty paces Almoſt in the middle of which
" ſtand two pyramids, each fifty paces above
" water, and as much below, in all, an
" hundred paces, there being upon each a
" Coloſſus, ſetting in a chair The water of
" this lake is not eſteemed to ſpring in the
" place (the ſoil being very dry) but comes out
" of the Nile by a trench, flowing ſix months
" into the lake, and ebbing as many into the
" Nile, yielding into the king's treaſury, for
" the fiſh taken therein, a talent of ſilver,
" for every day of the ſix months ebb, and
" twenty minæ when it flows The Egyp-
" tians would have it believed, that this lake
" was made by ſkill, on account of the
" iſland, and pyramids in it and where it is
" objected, that there is no ſign of earth, or
" out, they ſay that it was thrown into the
" river Nile "

After him alſo king Seſoſtris, returning vic
torious out of Aſia, * and " bringing with him
" a multitude of people out of the conquered
" countries, obliged them to dig ſeveral water
" courſes, which are ſtill in Egypt, impro-
" vidently making the country, which before
" was paſſable with horſe and waggon, to want
" that convenience for from that time,
" though Egypt is all plain, yet can neither
" horſe nor waggon paſs, by reaſon of the cuts,
which

---

‖ Plin v 9 § Herod. l ii c. 17 † Strab p. 788 C
† Herod l ii cap 13 ‡ Herodotus out lived Artaxerxes
Longimanus, king of Perſia Myris, or Mœris, reigned
in the tenth century after the flood

‡ Herod. lib ii c 137 † l ii c 149 * lib ii c 107

" which are many and various  But the reason
" why he fo trenched the country, was, that
" the cities more remote from the river might
" not want water to drink, upon the recefs of
" the ftream "

There were alfo very remarkable canals on
the Arabian fide of Egypt. a " As that at Pe-
" lufium, which fills the two lakes, that have
" their name from the fens there, befides other
" lakes and canals into them, in thofe parts,
" without Delta, and two others which
" meet in a lake in the Sethroitique divifion  "

For Egypt was by Sefoftris divided into
xxxvi parts, in Greek, NOMOI in Englifh you
may call them *Shires*  but that is the moft famous  canal, which was drawn into the Red
Sea.

It was firft undertaken b by king Nechoh the
fon of Pfammitichus, (this is that Pharaoh Nechoh, king of Egypt, who flew Jofiah, king
of Judah in battle c at Megiddo) being fecond-
ed by Darius, king of Perfia d " The length
" of this canal was four days fail  the breadth
" fuch that two gallies might row together  The
" water of Nile entered into it a little above the
" city of Bubaftis, and paffing by Patumos
" (a city of Arabia) entered the Red Sea. They
" began to dig in the plain of Egypt, towards
" Arabia, running a great way, from weft to
" eaft, by the foot of that hill, near Memphis,
" in which is the ftone quarry : then turning
" fouth, through the parting of the hill, into
" the Arabian gulf  The paffage from mount
" Caffius and the North Sea, unto the Red Sea,
" is a thoufand furlongs  but by this canal,
" the way was longer, being not fo ftraight.
" In the digging hereof there perifhed an hun-
" dred and twenty thoufand Egyptians  Nechoh
" having half done, defifted, being difcour-
" aged by an oracle, which faid, he wrought
" for the Barbarians  fo the Egyptians call all
" thofe, who ufe not their language "

Strabo e (who lived under Tiberius) fays,
that " this water-courfe iffued into the Red
" Sea, or Arabian gulf, at the city of Ar-
" cinoe, which fome call Cleopatris, and that
" it had paffed through thofe lakes, which are
" called *Bitter*." (They had the name of

*Marah, a* becaufe the children of Ifrael, at their
departure out of Egypt, could not drink of
thofe waters)  But the water of thofe lakes,
though in old time *bitter*, b " was changed, upon
" the making of this new river, and mingling
" with frefh water; now bred good fifh, and
" abundance of water fowl."  He fays, that
" this canal was firft made by Sefoftris, before
" the Trojan war; or (as others relate) it was
" only begun by the fon of Pfammitichus, who
" foon died.  Afterwards it was again re-
" fumed by Darius the Firft, who having al-
" moft finifhed the work, gave it over, out of
" an opinion, that the Red Sea was higher
" than Egypt. and that, if the whole ifthmus
" were cut, Egypt would be drowned with the
" fea  But the Ptolemies, kings of Egypt,
" cut it through, and fet a fluice upon the
" canal, that they might fail out into the fea,
" and in again, as they pleafed. c It was an
" hundred cubits in breadth, and deep enough
" for a great fhip."

*Could this noble, and once navigable canal, be
again opened, what an eafy and fpeedy communication would it afford to the Eaft-Indies ? inftead of
that dangerous circumnavigation, by either a
North-weft, or even a North-eaft paffage, fo often,
and hitherto fo fruitlefsly attempted, at fuch an im-
menfe expence.  But the misfortune is, this country
now is in the poffeffion of the Turks, or other nations,
totally ignorant of the advantages, arifing from
fuch a communication, and therefore it might be
expedient for the Eaft-India company, or fome fuch
opulent fociety, to turn their thoughts towards the
attaining fo defireable an object*

The intended benefit of this canal, feems
to have been an intercourfe between the
Mediterranean, and the Atlantic, and a communication of traffic, by water, between Europe,
and the Eaft-Indies.  but I do not find, that
any great ufe was made thereof to that purpofe;
for in after-times, the way of trading into thofe
eaftern parts, was either from the port of Gaza,
to Aila, a port town fituate near the bottom of
the Arabian gulf, on the eaft fide thereof, or
from Coptus, a town of Egypt, on this fide
Thebes, to Berenice, a port on the weft fide of
the Red Sea

" This

B

a Strab p 804  b Herod. l. ii c 158. c 2 Kings xxiii 27
d Herod. ut fupra e Lib xvii p. 804 B.        a Exod. xv. 23.  b Strab ib  c Ibid. p. 805.

" This paffage, from Gaza to Aila, *a* " is faid to be 1260 furlongs There are two " ways, one through Arabia, the other through " Egypt by Heroopolis, to which the nearer " courfe is by Pelufium, the way through the " deferts and fands, is going by camels, and " is obnoxious to ferpents "

From this town of Eloth, *b* Solomon made his voyage to Ophir It was loft in king Joram's reign, *c* when the Edomites revolted, but was recovered by Azariah, and under Ahaz *d* was taken by *e* Rezin king of Syria It was a frontier town of the Roman empire, and the ftations of the Tenth legion *f*

The other paffage from Coptus to Berenice, is reckoned 258 miles, the particular ftations of which you have in the Itinerary of Antoninus " They were fettled, *g* and inns erected by " Philadelphus, becaufe the innermoft part " of the Red Sea was not fo navigable This " Coptus was a neutral town, common both to " the Egyptians and Arabians, and the mart " for all Indian, Arabic and Ethiopic articles, " from whence was a canal cut into the Nile," *h* through which the merchandizes were tranf ported to Alexandria. Which place being, from the Macedonian times, the head of all Egypt, ought not flightly to be paffed over, becaufe none ever had the like advantage of artificial water-courfes, by which in a fhort time it became, for greatnefs, popularity, wealth, and pleafantnefs, one of the moft renowned cities in the world

The Egyptians fuperftitiouƒly abhorred the fea, and held all thofe in difefteem who got their living by it. And although according to the chronology of *i* Eufebius, they had the dominion of the fea, in the reigns of Ptamminis and Bocchoris, a little before the firft Olympiad (which was not fuitable to the diftracted condition of Egypt in thofe times,) *k* yet it is certain, that the Egyptians never had any fea-port, that Ptammitichus *l* was the firft king who admitted ftrangers to inhabit, that Naucratis (on the canal of Canopus) the only mart town of Egypt, was opened by Amafis, who took Cyprus, and died the fame year that Egypt was conquered by the Perfians

Neither was the coaft of Egypt fit for navigation, *m* " being without harbours, low, and

" full of flats and fhelves, except where the " ifland of Pharus, lying in length before a " bay, at a village called Rhacotis, an hundred " and thirty furlongs from Canopus, afforded " a moderate haven, of which neither the " Egyptians, nor the Perfians made any ufe, but " kept a guard there, to ward off ftrangers : " However, Alexander the Great, feeing the " convenience of the place, caufed a city to be " built there, which bore his name, the foun- " dation of which was laid with bran, inftead " of chalk, which was taken for a good omen "

This city ftands as it were between two feas ; having on the fouth the lake Mareia, or Mareotis but it would have been a great inconvenience to have dwelt in a dry country, fo far from the river Nile, had not that difadvantage been avoided by means of artificial rivers therefore that navigable canal was made from Canopus, *a* which became famous for the luxury of its inhabitants

Another navigable river was likewife made from the haven, *b* on the Mediterranean, to the faid lake Mareotis *c* " This lake is filled from " the Nile by many canals, as well from above" that is, or the lake Meris, of which I have fpoken, " as on the fides of it " by canals, cut immediately from the Nile, and having eight iflands in it, " contains above 150 fur- " longs in breadth, and near 300 in length, " being well inhabited round about, and afford- " ing good corn, *d* by which water-paffages, " more articles were brought to Alexandria, " than by fea ; ƒ as the haven on the lake fide " was richer than that on the fea, and more " goods carried from Alexandria to Italy, than " from Italy thither, as plainly appears by the " veffels, more or lefs freighted, which pafs " from thence, and from Puteoli. Befides the " wealth that is brought in at both havens from " the lake and fea, the goodnefs of the air is " not unworthy to be noticed, it being occafion- " ed by the water on both fides of the city, and " the feafonable rifing of the river Nile for " whereas other towns, fituate by lakes, have " in the heat of fummer a grofs and ftifling air, " their banks being left muddy, flimy exhala- " tions are drawn up by the fun, which render " the air unwholfome, and occafion ficknefs in " the

*a* Strab l xvi p. 759 *b* 2 Chron viii 18 *c* 2 Kings viii. 20 *d* ib xiv 22 *e* b xvi 6 *f* S Heron. de locis *g* Strab l xvii p 815 *h* ib p 798 C *i* An 1230 *k* Herod l. ii *l* ib c 178 *m* Strab l xvii p 791

*a* Strab p 800 *b* ib 793, 795, A. *c* Ib, p 799 C *d* ib, p 793 A

" the beginning of the summer, the Nile being
" full, replenishes the lake, and leaves no part
" muddy, to exhale any malignant vapours:
" at which time, the Etesian winds blow from
" the North Sea, so that the Alexandrians pass
" the summer very pleasantly "

And that the improvements made in Egypt
by the drains and new rivers, after the building
of Alexandria, was very large, as appears by
these following instances, in several ages   " In
" the sacred *a* commentaries of the antient
" priests, there were numbered in Egypt cities
" and towns of note, eighteen thousand. Under
" Amasius (the last king before the Persian
" Conquest,) there were twenty thousand towns
" in Egypt *b* inhabited   And under Ptolemy
" the first, above thirty thousand "

The printed copies of Diodorus have only three
thousand, but that reading is faulty as appears
by the preceding numbers, and the testimony
of Theocritus, *c* who was one of the seven Plei-
ades in the court of Philadelphus, the second
Ptolemy, in whose territories there were thirty
three thousand, three hundred and thirty-nine,
the improvement seeming then to be more compleat

However, in tract of time, through great
neglect, these cuts and drains, by which the
overflowings of the Nile so much inriched this
country, filted up   but Augustus Cæsar *d* having reduced Egypt to a Roman province, cau-
sed them to be scoured by his soldiers, which
noble work did so much restore it to the fertility
it formerly enjoyed, and consequently increase
the populousness of the country, that the number of inhabitants, over and above the Alexandrians, were shortly after found to be no less
than seven million, and five hundred thousand, as the collecting the tribute money *e*
shewed. And thus much for Egypt

## CHAP. II.

## BABYLON.

I am now come to that famous city of Babylon,
built in a low, flat country, of which Sir
Walter Raleigh *f* gives a reason, why there is

so little written of Belus, who succeeded Nim-
rod, the first Assyrian monarch) says, that it
is thought he spent much of his time in draining the low lands of Babylon, and drying and
making firm grounds of all those great fens
and over-flown marshes, which adjoined to it.

How the parts hereabouts came to be thus
surrounded, let us hear what Pliny says, *a* which
is this in effect.   The river Euphrates being cut
into parts, stretches its left arm into Mesu-
potamia;  by Seleucia, the principal city in
Syria, and so into the Tigris  and its right
branch to Babylon, the chief city of Chaldæa,
whence, passing through the midst of that country, it runs into the fens   It is reported, that
this division of that river was made by Gobaris
the præfect, lest by its violent course, it
might have infested the city of Babylon  but by
the Assyrians it is called *Nearmalcha*, which
signifies the kingly river

That the inundations from this river are occasioned by effects, the same as those of the
Nile, before spoken of, we have not only the
testimony of the above mentioned *b* Strabo,
whose words are these,   " Exundat enim
" Euphrates æstate, sub ver incipiens, &c *c*
" Euphrates overflows in summer, beginning
" at the spring-time, when the snow in Arme-
" nia is dissolved, so that the fields are over-
" flowed with water, unless that the flood is
" diverted by canals, in such a manner as to re-
" strain the river Nile in Egypt; on which ac-
" count canals are dug," &c

That the banks and drains made by Belus
did not fully answer that work of draining the
low lands, or in case it did, that after-ages,
through discontinuance of their repair, were
little the better for them, appears by the relation of Herodotus, *d* who speaking of two famous queens of Babylon, viz Semiramis, and
Nitocris, says of Semiramis, (who reigned five
ages before the other)  " Hæc per planitiem ag-
" geres exstruxit, spectando dignos, quum
" antehac flumen eam restagnare solitum," *e*
" She raised banks throughout the whole level,
" worthy of observation, whereas, before she
" did so, it was wont to be inundated by the
" river "

B 2                                    And

---

*a* Diod Sic p 19 B  *b* Herod l ii c 177.  *c* Theoc
Idyl xvii ver 82  *f* Suet i Aug cap 18  *e* Joseph de
bello l ii c 16  *f* Hist of the World, l i cap 10 sect 4

*c* C Plin Nat Hist lib v c 26.  *b* Ib lib v c 6
Ib l v c 26  *c* Strab lb xi p 740  *d* Herod l i.

And of Nitocris, who *a* being more activ and diligent than her predeceffor, "ante omni a " fluvium Euphratem," &c In the firft place " fhe diverted the current of the Euphrates " into winding canals, which before ran in a " ftrait courfe, through the middle of the city, " levelling the ditches above, fo that it might " thrice flow into Arderica, a certain village of " Affyria, and that thofe things which were " conveyed by the fea towards Babylon, through " the river Euphrates, fhould thrice land at " this village, for three days together This " fhe accomplifhed And likewife upon the " verge of the faid river on each fide, fhe railed " banks, of a prodigious fize and height

"Moreover, far above the city, and at fome " diftance from the river, fhe dug a channel " for the fen, as deep as the water. which was " in breadth every way, near three hundred and ' twenty furlongs. and the earth dug out of it " fhe brought to the banks of the river, the fi es " of which fhe ftrengthened with ftone, in fuch " places, where the weight of the faid banks did " opprefs them. Thefe two works, *viz.* the " turning of the river into that winding courfe, " and the making that drain, fhe did: firft, to " the end that the faid river, by the many wind- " ings of which it might glide more gently, " next, that paffages for fhips towards Babylon " might be mæandering; and laftly, that by " thefe navigations the long turnings of the " canal might be fupported."

## CHAP. III.

## GREECE.

I Next come to thofe works of this kind, which were performed by the Greeks, of which I fhall give an inftance, in Theffaly and Acarnania. *b* The firft of thefe is faid to have been antiently a lake, being on every fide inclofed with mountains· for on the eaft it is bounded by the hills Pelion and Offa, mutually joining at their defcent, to the north, Olympus; to the weft, Pindus, and to the fouth, Othrys The valley between thefe Hills is called Theffaly. Among other rivers that flow into it,

thefe five are the chief, Peneus, Apidanus, Onochonus, Enipeus, and Pamifus, which, running from the hills incompaffing this country, unite in the plain, and become one ftream, which at one paffage, and that but narrow, difembogues into the fea. from the confluence of thefe waters, Peneus continues the name.

It is reported, *a* that in old time, when there as yet was no out-let, thefe rivers, and the lake Bæbeis befides, were not called as at prefent, although they did run no lefs than now; but in their courfe made all Theffaly a fea. The Theffalians themfelves affirm, that Neptune made that paffage, by which Peneus flows into the fea for the Greeks afcribe all beneficial inventions to their Gods. and Herodotus fuppofes it was the effect of an earthquake : but no man can deny it to be a very remarkable work of Draining. And that it is now a place of extraordinary beauty, I fhall refer my reader to the map of Tempe, in Ortelius's Parergon.

Of Acarnania this is obfervable, *b* that where Achelous runs into the fea, it has already made continent one half of the iflands, called Echinades and that the fable relates, *c* that Hercules here encountering with Achelous, who is faid to have transformed himfelf into a bull, becaufe of the roaring noife of the river, broke off one of his horns, and gave it to Oeneus in pledge of his marriage with Dejanira his daughter Thofe who collect truth out of fables, fay, that Hercules, who was generally beneficial, for Oeneus, his father-in-law's fake, reftrained the exorbitant overflowings of this river, with banks, and canals, and drained a great part of the adjacent country, and that this was the Cornucopia, which the poets made to be the emblem of plenty.

## CHAP. IV.

## Of the ROMANS.

T HAT the Roman works of this nature were not a few, and thofe very eminent, I fhall next proceed to fhew, by their drains in the Pompeian marfhes, the Foffa Mariana, the

the improvements about Placentia, and Gallia Cisalpina; the restraint of the river Tiber in its overflowings, and the exsiccation of the great Fucine lake in Italy.

## SECT. I.

### The POMPEIAN MARSHES.

In the year 593, when L. Anicius Gallus and M Cornelius Cethegus were Consuls, the Senate, a being in council concerning the Provinces, because there seemed not sufficient use against the enemy for the ordinary forces of both the Consuls (which were four legions, besides the auxiliaries, & socii,) there was a motion made, concerning the improvement of a great level of waste land, lying under water, about forty miles from Rome, b in Latium. Which business was entertained with great approbation; for, as it is esteemed a high commendation for a private man to be called a good husbandman, by the Consuls; so did the Senate now think, that they should deserve the name of good husbands for the commonwealth, if, on this opportunity they could gain such a quantity of rich land to Italy, which is for the greatest part mountainous and barren.

Neither was this employment thought too mean for the legions, though consisting of free men for the Roman and Italian infantry, being as well accustomed to the spade and basket, as to the sword and buckler, used to be their own pioneers, in their daily intrenchments. neither did they work for their own safety only, in time of danger, but for the common good likewise, in time of security. c The Consuls, anno 566, had herein given a precedent, who, lest their soldiers should be idle, employed them in making public roads, hereupon it was decreed, that one Consul should attend the enemy in Gaul, and the other undertake the draining of the Pompeian Marshes

All the country, d which lies eastward of Rome, between the river Tiber, and Campania, is now united, under the name of Latium, and that place which lies towards the sea, beneath the range of hills, which reach from Belitre

to Terracina, is the largest It is named from Suessa Pometia, antiently a rich city, and metropolitan of the Volsci, but now scarce extant. The maritime parts of this vale, for a great extent, are drowned, not so much through any inundation of the sea, whose tides are here but small, as by reason the waters of Amasenus and Ufens the larger river, having not their passage sufficiently open unto the sea, diffuse themselves over those spacious low grounds, up towards Sulmo and Setia This tract is therefore called the Pomentin, or Pomptin Fens, having been in such manner surrounded beyond all memory; for Homer, describing the arrival of Ulysses at the Circean promontory, a calls it an island, in regard of these waters on the one side, and sea on the other the which island (says Theophrastus) had about ten miles of circuit· But in his time, for he wrote b about twenty years after Appius had been Censor, the rivers, by continually bringing down soil, had joined it to the continent So that I do not perceive how the Romans were lords of the country, or since there had been any order taken for the gaining this ground from the water. But now, by order of the Senate, the Pomptin Fens were laid dry by Cornelius Cethegus, c the Consul, to whom that province fell, and they were made good ground.

The country people, allured by the fertility of the soil, settled themselves here in such abundance, that there was said to be, not long after this time, three and twenty d towns in this place; it being a land capable of many thousand husbandmen. But e in after-times, whilst the state (distracted with civil wars) neglected the maintenance of the banks, the waters again, by degrees, gained upon the land; f so that Julius Cæsar had an intention, not only to have drained the fens anew, but to have brought the Appian way across them.

Whether Augustus did any thing to them, may be doubted, for in Vespasian's time g they were come to that pass, that it was esteemed a miracle, they should ever have been so well inhabited. At the same time, when the beds of the rivers were scoured, and the lands canaled, was

a Liv xliii. 915, 922. b Plin. l. xviii, c. 3. ex Catone. c Liv l. xxxix. d Stab l. v.

a Odyss l x ver 158 b Ann 460 Plin iii 5. c Liv Epist xix Florus, lib xlvi. d Plin l iii c e Mucino, sui ævi e Plutarch Cæs p 745 C f Dio, xlii p 272 D. g Plin. iii. 5.

was that great cut made through the midst of these fens, which ſerved afterwards, not ſo much for a ſewer, as for the more direct and eaſy paſſage of the traveller. for whereas the Appian way (tracing the up land) turned eaſtward, and went in compaſs about the fens, this, being drawn in a ſtraight line, croſſes over more directly, and joins the highway again. About three miles from Terracina, ſays Strabo, *a* as you go to Rome, this canal abutteth on the Appian way, and is repleniſhed in many places with the fen, and river waters. The ordinary paſſage is in the night, ſo they who go aboard in the evening, land in the morning, and proceed the reſt of their journey on the Appian way. They paſs alſo in the day time, the boats being towed by mules. Which water paſſage is elegantly deſcribed by Horace, *b* where the company parting, he mentions the two ways from Forum Appii, to Terracina, the Appian, and this by boat.

This landing-place next to Rome, was in after-times known by the name of Forum Appii, a ſmall town inhabited chiefly by water-men *c* and victuallers. but it is not evident, whether it was formerly built, when the Appian way was firſt made, or whether now, upon this occaſion, it was erected for the convenience of them that here took water, and named from the road on which it ſtands. The uſe of this paſſage continued long after the reſtagnation of the fens, which were not again drained, till the time of Trajan the Emperor (performing the work, which Julius Cæſar perhaps intended) made a ſtone cauſe-way through the Pomptin fens, building ſeveral inns, and moſt magnificent bridges, *d* for the conveyance of ſuch waters as were ſpread on the upper part of the fen; in memory of which a monumental ſtone was erected, with this inſcription, copied from the original at Terracina, by that learned gentleman, Mr John Graves:

```
        IMP   CAESAR
        DIVI  NERVAE
        FILIVS  NERVA
        TRAIANVS  AVG
         GERMANICVS
          DACICVS
        PONTII  MAX
         TRIB POT XIIII
        IMP VI  COS V PP
      a XVIII SILICE SVA PECVNIA
            STRAVIT
            ̅LI̅I̅
```

This work of Trajan's had no peculiar name, but becauſe it ſhortened the Appian way, was eſteemed a part of it. yet about four hundred years after, from the number of mile-ſtones, it was called Decennovium, reckoning from Forum Appii ad Medias *b* (the lodging of Trajan reared on the way) ix miles, from thence to Terracina, x more. and the canal, or river ſo called, becauſe it was xix miles long. After this, Theodoricus, king of Italy, *c* authorized one Decius *c* to drain Paludem Decennovii. which he performed by cutting many canals, that were not before. this being the third and laſt time, that theſe marſhes were laid dry, and in memory thereof, cauſed *d* this inſcription to be ſet up. which is given in the following page.

*Anxuri,*

---

*a* Strab l. v p 235 B    *b* Lib. 1 Sat. v.    *c* Ibid. ver v   *d* Dio, l lxiii. p 777

*a* Decennovium.   *b* Itin Hieroſolym.   *c* Procop de B Goth l 1 182. *d* Caſſiod Var l 11 Ep 32, 33

*Anxuri*, five *Terracinæ*, in *Cæfaret* templo.

DN. GLORIOSIS ADQ IN.
CLVTVS. REX THEODORICVS VICT
AC. TRIF SEMPER. AVG BONO. REIP.
NATVS CVSTOS. LIBERTATIS ET.
PROPAGATOR. ROMANI. NOMINIS,
DOMITOR GENTIVM.

DECENNOVII VIAE APPIAE ID EST. A TRIP.
VSQ TERRACENAM ITER AD LOCA QVAE.
CONFLVENTIBVS AB VTRAQ PARTE PALVDVM
PER OMNES RETRO-PRINCIPIVM INVNDAVERVNT
VSVI. PVBLICO ET SECVRITATI VIANTIVM
ADMIRANDA PROPITIO DEO FELICITATE,
RESTITVIT OPERI INIVNCTO NAVITER INSVDANTE.
ADQ CLEMENTIS-IMI PRINCIPIS FELICITER
DESERVIENTE PRAECONIIS FX PROSAPIA DECIO
RVM CAEC. MAV BASILIO DECIO VC $\overline{INL}$
EXPF VRB EXPPO FX CONS ORD PAT QVI AD
PERPETVANDAM TANTI DOMINI GLORIAM PER
PLVRIMOS QVI ANTE ERANT ALBEOS - - - - - -
- - - - - - - - - - - - - - - - - - DEDVCTA in MA
RE AQVA IGNOTAE AIAVIS ET NIMIS ANTIQVE.
REDDI - - - - - - - - - - - - - - -

## SECT. II.

### FOSSA MARIANA.

This was made by the famous Marius *a* (who was feven times conful) near one of the out-falls of the great river Rhodanus, in that fenny and muddy country, not far from Arles, and entering into the fea

## SECT III.

### The Fens about PLACENTIA.

Thefe being occafioned by the overflowings of the Po, *b* were drained by Scaurus, who caufed navigable canals to be cut from them, to Parma The like is ftill obfervable in the territory of Ferria, which, though a low ground, and receiving the current of Po, with other rivers of Lombardy, is yet fecured by banks and works, which hinder their inundations, particularly by the help of the Rotto di Ficirollo, and the Ramo di Poliftella

## SECT. IV.

### GALLIA CISALPINA.

This country abounds with rivers, efpecially that territory belonging to the Venetians, which lving flat, and towards the fea, by the flowing of the tides became a fenny marfh but by the help of canals and banks, ( in fuch manner as was long before experienced in the lower Egypt ) fome part of which has been drained, and made ufeful for tillage, *a* fome navigable, and fome cut into iflands

## SECT. V

### Of the River TIBER

To reftrain the exorbitant overflowings of this ftream, which was not a little choaked with mud and feveral old buildings, which had fallen into it, I find, that Auguftus Cæfar *b* beftowed fome coft in cleaning and fcouring it And that,

*a* Plutarch in vita C Marii, ect Lutetix 1624, p 413 414 Ære Chrifti Ina nat an 65  *b* Strab l v p. Tacit l i

*a* Strab l v p 212  *b* Sueton in Aug c 30, Annal

that, after this, through abundance of rain, the low grounds about the city, fuffering much by great inundations, the remedy in preventing the like for the future, was, by the Emperor Tiberius, committed to the care of Ateius Capito, and L. Aruntius. Whereupon it was by them debated in the fenate, Whether for the moderating the floods of this river, the ftreams and lakes, by which it increafed, fhould be diverted another way: But to that propofal there were feveral objections made, from many cities and colonies, the Florentines defiring, that the Glanis might not be put out of its ufual channel, and turned into the river Arnus; in regard, much prejudice would thereby be incurred. In like manner did the inhabitants of Terano argue; affirming, that if the river Far fhould be cut into fmaller ftreams, the overflowings of it would furround the moft fruitful grounds of Italy. Neither were thofe of Reate, a city in Umbria, filent, who refufed to ftop the paffage of the lake Velinus, (now called Lago de Terni) into the faid river Nar. The bufinefs, therefore, finding this oppofition, was deferred; After which a Nerva or Trajan attempted likewife, by a canal, to prevent the fatal inundations of this river; but without fuccefs.

## S E C T. VI.

### The Fucine Lake.

Nor is it a little to be admired, what labour and cofts the Romans beftowed in attempts of this kind, it being teftified of the Emperor Claudius, b that he employed no lefs than thirty thoufand men, for the fpace of eleven years, without intermiffion, for draining the great Fucine lake, in Italy c who dug for that purpofe, a channel of three miles in length, part of which was cut through a mountain, yet did not accomplifh the work. Which failing, by no means deterred pofterity from making farther attempts therein: for it appears, that Pliny defcribed to the Emperor Trajan, d how it might be perfected. What he did thereupon I find not, for it was his fucceffor Adrian e who finifhed it.

## C H A P. V.

### The Belgic Provinces

FROM the works of the Romans, in Italy, I now come to the Belgic provinces. This country was part of Gaul; but fo full of woods and fens, that the victorious Cæfar could not conquer it

—— "Omnes Gallias, nifi quæ paludibus invia fuere, ut Salluftio docetur autore, poft decennales belli mutuas clades, Cæfar focietati noftræ fœderibus junxit æternis," a fays Am. Marcellinus; (i e.) "All France, except the fenny parts, which are not paffable, after ten years war, was by Cæfar reduced." "And afterwards fays farther, "b Hæ verò Galliæ," &c. But thefe parts of Gaul being, by reafon of the fens, unpaffable, are the province of the Menapii, whom he thought had been terrified with his other warlike atchievements, and eafy to be conquered, though he had fubdued none of them: however, they, not dwelling in towns, but in cottages, in fenny places furrounded with thick woods, having hidden whatever they had moft valuable, did more annoyance to the wearied Romans, than they received from them." 'Tis true, that Cæfar cutting down the woods, did attempt to pafs the faid fens, but by reafon of their greatnefs, and that the winter feafon approached, defpairing of fuccefs, he forbore the enterprize

Now, that this part of Gaul, here fpoken of, is the fame which we at this day call Flanders, we have the teftimony of a late learned writer. c "Quamvis in Flandriâ fuiffet hic author," &c (fays he) "If this author had been himfelf in Flanders, and made a ftrict ocular furvey of that country, he could not more exactly have defcribed it, as it antiently was: for the Nervii and Attrebates, firft met with vaft woods, about Gant, Ipres, and Cortrav, even to Bruges, and afterwards having paffed the woods, with mighty fens, where now the territory of Franc——, Furne, and Berge, are, extending to the main ocean."

It

---

a Plin. l. viii Epift. 17    b Sueton. in vitâ Claudii, cap. 20    c Now Lago de Celano    d C. Plin. Ep. l. x 69 n    e Ælius Spart. de Adriano Cæf. in Hift. Auguft. Parif. edit. anno. 1620.

a Lib. xv.    b Ibid. l. xxxix    c Olivarius Uredius, in Hift. Com. Flandr. de vet. Flaand. cap. 1. p. 3

It is the opinion, therefore of some learned men, that it has received its name from the watery and fenny situation. And Uredius taking notice of Kilianus (a) his exposition of the word *ulacke*, that it signifies " æstuarium, locus " viciffim æstu maris, vel nudus, vel aquis stag- " nantibus offertus ," id est, " a place where- " unto, either the sea-tides do ebb and flow, or " that is filled with standing waters " has this " expreffion ·——Adeoque, quia toto illo ti- " ctu, ab Ardenburgo Dixmudam ufque et " ultra, plura ejufmodi aquofa loca et paludofa " occurrebant, tota regio Ulaendren dicta, undè " Flandræ, numero plurali, voce in latinita- " tem deflexâ " i e " Therefore becaufe in " that whole tract, from Ardenburg to Dixmuth, " and beyond, there are many of thofe watery " and fenny places, all the country is called " Ulaendren, and thence Flanders, in the plu- " ral number, the word being adopted into " Latin."

Much more could I add, from the authority of authentic hiftorians, to manifeft how full of marfhes, lakes, and fens, this country antient- ly has been, were it needful, though now there is little appearance that ever it was fo, for by the induftry of the inhabitants, thofe fens and marfhes are fo banked and drained, that the fertility of that tract, has made it one the moft rich and populous countries in that part of the world

There are thofe who affirm, that Baldwin the Firft, (b) having wedded Judith, daughter to the Emperor Charles the Bald, who was alfo king of France, had by the gift of the faid king, this territory of Flanders, of which he was made earl and that this Baldwin, befides his build- ing the caftle of Bruges, and other places of ftrength, did much in clearing of the woods and exficcation of the marfhes, for making the country more habitable and fruitful. That this is undoubtedly true, I am induced to believe, from what the learded Uredius, before-menti- oned, fays, viz. "——Eo anno, fc. DCCCXIII. " & anno fequenti, Baldvinus operam adhi- " buit Brugenfi caftro & vico, aquis & firmi- " tatibus muniendis, adverfus Normannos, ex " Edictis Synodi Piftenfis anno DCCCLXII & DCCCLXIII. quæ habentur in Capitulis Caroli

" Calvi, editis à Sirmondo——ut illi qui in " hoftem pergere non potuerint juxta anti- " quam, & aliarum gentium confuetudinen, ad " civitates novas, & pontes, ac tranfitus palu- " dum operentur, & in civitate atque in mar- " châ muactas, faciant ad defenfionem patriæ, " omnes fine ullâ excufatione veniant." " i.e. In " the year DCCCLXII and the year following, " Baldwin beftowed labour in fortifying the " caftle and town of Bruges, with moats and " bulwarks, againft the Normans, by virtue of " the edicts of the Piftenfian fynod, held in the " year DCCCLXII and DCCCLXIII which are re- " corded in the ftatutes of Charles the Bald, " publifhed by Sirmondus, viz. that thofe who " were not able to march againft the enemy, " fhould, according to the antient cuftom of " other nations, be employed in making of new " cities, bridges, and paffages over the fens : " and, without any excufe, fhould come to " raife banks in the cities and limits of the coun- " try, for the defence thereof "

The ftory of draining that part of this coun- try, lying betwixt Dam and Ardenburgh, and thereby making it habitable, being very me- morable, and much to the honour of thofe who were active in that work, I fhall in the next place exhibit.

In the year MCLXIX. (a) Floris earl of Hol- land, demanding the ifle of Walchren, in Zee- land, from Philip earl of Flanders. After a war between them, upon this quarrel, they came to an accommodation, viz. That Count Philip fhould enjoy to himfelf and his heirs for ever, the land of Waes, (which is one of the beft quarters of Flanders, which the earls of Hol- land had formerly held) and Floris to be reftored to the faid ifle of Walchren, in confideration of which, he fhould fend to count Philip a thoufand men, expert in making of drains, to ftop the breach, which had been made near unto Dam, or the Slufe ; whereby the country was drowned by every high fea, the which the Flemings could by no means fill up, neither with wood, nor any other matter, for that all funk as in a gulf without any bottom ; whereby in procefs of time, Bruges and all that jurifdic- tion had been in danger of being loft by inun- dation, and to become all fea, if it were not

C speedily

---

a Olivarius Uredius, in Hift Com. Flandr. de vet Fland. cap i. p 9. b Munft Cofmog lib, ii p 119

a Hift. of the Netherlands, p. 14 & 15.

speedily remedied. Whereupon count Floris sent the best workmen he could find, who being come to the place, found a great hole, near this dam; and at the entrance a sea dog, that for six days together, did nothing but cry and howl very terribly. They not knowing what this might signify, resolved to cast this dog into that hole; whereupon a mad-headed Hollander, getting into the bottom of the dyke, took the dog by the tail, and cast him into the midst of the gulf, with earth and turf after him, so that finding a bottom they filled it up, by little and little.

And because many workmen, that came in to the repairing of this work, lodged in cabbins (which made the place seem a pretty town) count Philip gave to them, and such others as would inhabit there, as much land as they could recover, from Dam to Ardenburg, for them and their successors for ever, with many immunities and freedoms; by reason of which many planted themselves there, and in process of time made it a spacious town, the which, by reason of this dog so cast into the hole, they named Hondtsdam; that is to say, a dog's sluice; Dam in Flemish signifying a sluice, and Hondt, a dog; and therefore, at this day, the said town now called Dam, bears a dog in their arms.

After this, *viz* in the year of Christ MCLXXX were the banks from (*a*) Dam to Sluse (then called Lamminsuliet) raised and made; by which means the sea, which had drowned all the tract, was excluded.

I now descend to HOLLAND and ZEELAND.

---

## CHAP. VI.

## HOLLAND.

THIS country, consisting of a three-fold earth, *viz.* sandy to the sea, clay to the rivers, and moorish in other places, is accounted, saith (*b*) Bertius, not without good reason, to be the gift of the ocean, and of the rivers Rhene and Mose, as Egypt is of the river Nile, by the testimony of Herodotus. Consonant to which, is that expression of (*a*) Petr. Nannius——
" Quod si penitùs liceat in origines nostras inquirere, omnino mihi persuadeo, Hollandiam munus Boreæ ac Rheni esse," &c. i. e.
" If it be at all lawful to inquire into our origin, I wholly persuade myself, that Holland is the gift of the north-wind, and of the river Rhene: and was in the beginning no other than a more high place than ordinary, over which the tides did usually flow, whereby, through the increase of the sands, which the north-wind fiercely agitating the waves) accumulated it first became a shore, and afterwards raised those sandy heaps, which we daily see, both to be made and destroyed" And farther added, " that the waters of the Rhene, by this stop, being kept up as it were with a bank, settled the soil, brought down by the stream, about the shores, and so, by long and frequent inundations, produced those pastures. (*b*) For it cannot be imagined, says Bertius, that the face of this country was always as it now appears, or that it soon arose from it's former condition, to this fertile and pleasant state, in which we behold it at present; there being much time, extraordinary labour, excessive study, vast expence, and great diligence necessary to produce such effects, nature therefore first inviting the inhabitants bordering near upon it, to make those banks of land, as a defence against the north wind, and necessity also spurring them on (than which no master is more ingenious or more powerful) in time, those their reiterated endeavours became a second nature to them, it being not unusual to see the very boys and girls, when they came to the sea-side to recreate themselves, by pulling off their shoes and stockings, and gathering up the sand to make walls against the ocean, within which thus encompassing themselves, they despise the force of the waves."

That the Batavians (a warlike and hardy people of Germany) were the first, who observing as well the natural richness of the soil, which the surges of the ocean had, by it's silt, sands, and

---

*a* Annales Flandr per Meierum.   *b* P. Bertius de aggeribus, &c. cap. xiii.

*a* Lib. x. Miscellan. cap i.    *b*. P. Bertius de agger.ous, c. xiii.

and mud, fo raifed in time, to the height of its ufual tides; did by their great induftry, in making large and ftrong banks, thus gain it from the fea, and make it habitable, we have the credit of feveral hiftorians: (a) as alfo that the Danes and Normans did, after their invafion continue to preferve what they found fo gained. Nay, I find that the Saxons, whom my author calls, " Aggerum exftruendorum peritos, fkilful in making fuch banks," did exercife their induftry in this kind, here, the town of Saxhenheym giving alfo fome teftimony to fuch an opinion. Nor is it unlikely, but that the Francs, whofe native feat thefe parts of the Netherlands was, contributed much to the works, here, of that kind, forafmuch as it is apparent, that they were the raifers of thofe banks upon the Loire in France, which do reftrain the inundations of that river from drowning the plains that lie adjacent to it. How much honour therefore is due to the memory of thofe induftrious people, who entered firft upon this great and profitable work, I cannot eafily exprefs for " invenire primum præcipuumque eft," &c fays (b) Polydore Verg i e " The firft invention " is the chief and principal thing, the fame of " which fo excited many, out of the love they " have to themfelves, that every one, were it " poffible, would be accounted the author of " fome art, becaufe without arts, it is evident " that there could be no living." To which may be added, the confideration of its difficulty, which makes it much the more worthy of regard.—" Quid enim laudis (fays, the before " mentioned author) affecutus effet Cæfar, fi " facile fuiffet Britannis bellum inferre? Aut " Hannibal, quantum gloriæ fibi comparâffet " fi pervias Alpes dum Italiam adiret, citra, ut " dicitur, pulverem, fudoremque, ac non " magnâ fuorum cæde feciffet? i e For what " had Cæfar got, if his war with the Britons " had been an eafy undertaking? or what glory " had Hannibal obtained, if he had paffed the " Alps with duft only and fweat, and not " without great flaughter of his foldiers?" Nor can I be filent in the due praife of their pofterity, through whofe induftry, not only

what hath been fo happily gained by their anceftors, is for the moft part kept and preferved: but befides the daily improvement thereof, through their fingular dexterity and diligence, much more, frequently, increafed and gained. To which end, and that thofe their defenfive walls may be the better maintained, they conftitute peculiar magiftrates, whofe charge and office it is to look to them, (a) whom they call Duickgraven, that by them, both the inner and outer banks may upon all occafions be repaired and made good, in cafe of any breach or decay in them. Which banks are of that ftrength and height, that they preferve the country from certain drowning at high tides, for it is evident to all who fail in the ports of thefe flat countries, that at full fea, the fields within the banks, in which feeding cattle are, and corn growing, do lie below the level of the ocean; which is to many no fmall aftonifhment.

Having thus fhewn how and by whom this country of Holland was firft gained and made habitable, I will now make fome obfervations on thofe advantages which have been farther acquired of late years, by this active and ingenious people, in their great and beneficial improvements, the number of the inhabitants fo much increafing, urgent neceffity enforced them to make ufe of their utmoft fkill, for the accomplifhing fomething that might be eminent in fuch a cafe. This was by draining feveral lakes, of which fixteen were moft confiderable, all this was performed within the fpace of the laft fifty years, by certain windmills, conftructed and erected for that purpofe. The chief of which lakes, called the Beemfter, containing about eighteen hundred acres made dry by the help of LXX of thofe mills, and walled about with a bank of great ftrength and fubftance, is now become a place of fuch profit and pleafure, through the abundance of cattle, that are fed in it, and the plantations therein, otherwife made, that it may, not without defert, be very juftly called, the moft famous garden of all that Province.

The other lakes, fo drained, as I have faid, are contiguous to the cities of Alcmare, Horne,

C 2 and

---

a Munft Cofm p 516. P Bertius ut fupra Ibid b De rerum invent. in Epift. fua ibidem. Ludovico Odaxio.

a P. Bertius, ut fupra.

and Purmerende; and are commonly called de Schermere, de Waert, de Purmer, and de Wormer: which, being drained by the help of fewer mills, are now become not only moſt fruitful paſtures, and little inferior to the Beemſter; but have ſo inriched the adjoining villages, by the concourſe of people to them, that through the great emolument to the public treaſury, and the abandance of cheeſe and butter there made, ſeems to be a new Holland ariſen within the old.

That the performance of theſe eminent works required extraordinary knowledge and ſkill, which antient times had not attained to, and foreign nations now admire, is not to be doubted: the engines of ſeveral kinds made uſe of in this buſineſs, for raiſing up the water, and caſting it off, being framed by men of ſingular judgements in mathematical learning, and ſuitable to the depth of the water, or proper for conveying it away

Neither have the attempts of theſe people, by the like commendable enterprizes, in South Holland, about the cities of Leyden, Dort, and Amſterdam, had leſs ſucceſs, there having been many thouſands of acres, formerly over-ſpread with water, made good and firm land, within theſe few years, by the help of theſe engines, as I have been credibly informed by that learned gentleman, Dr John Laet of Leyden. to whom I have been much beholden for what I have here ſaid, concerning theſe improvements in Holland.

---

# C H A P.  VII.

# F R I S E L A N D.

THIS country, ſituate alſo very low, and much ſubject to inundations from the ſea, wants not the like advantages by walls and banks for its better ſafeguard, as that of Holland, nor of leſs antiquity I preſume. But thoſe elder times I ſhall paſs by, and take notice of that remarkable and famous work, of this kind, done by (a) Gaſpar Robleſius (a Portugueſe)

Governor of this Province and Groningen, under Philip the ſecond, King of Spain.

About the year MDLXXVI. this worthy perſon, having driven out Entenius, a rebel and diſperſed his forces, applying himſelf to works and ſtudies befitting a time of peace, perfecting that famous ſea bank, by which, Weſtergoons, a part of that territory was defended from the overflowing of the ocean, which for many ages, had by its tides occaſioned infinite damage to the country; thereby raiſing to his memory a laſting monument of his fame, for by his contrivance it was, that the work was undertaken; and by his power, that the people, of themſelves averſe and ſlow to ſo public and beneficial a work, were compelled to come in, man by man, to raiſe this ſtrong bank, as if it had been to quench a fire. In this alone, it being a work of ſecurity to the country, and for his honour, which exceeded the renown of thoſe that had been the preceding governors of that country, under the Emperor Charles the Vth, and the ſaid King Philip, to laſt ſays my author, "quam-" diu natura rerum, aut mari limes ſit " i e. to the end of the world. For, this famous ſeabank being perfected, Adrianus Veſtartius, and Johannes Carolus went to Harling, and erected a monumental pillar of ſtone, upon the ſhore there, which ſhould give bounds to the maritime and midland Weſtergois, and from that time avoid all future contention about the repairing that ſea bank, in the foundation of which pillar were laid twelve thouſand bricks, the height of it being xx feet above the top of the ſaid ſeabank, and this inſcription towards the weſt.

" Caſpari á Robles equiti, domino de Billi
" &c Friſiæ, Groningæ, ejuſque territorii ac
" adjacentium gubernatori, quod hanc provin-
" ciam, præter arma, conſiliis & munimentis ju-
" verit, ac inter cætera aggere ipſis kal Nov.
" MDLXX. funditus everſo, ampliſſimi D Viglii
" Zuichemi, patris patriæ, auxiliaribus operis,
" & adhibits Igramo ab Achelen Pr Adriano
" vaſtaret, Petro Frittema, & Joanne Carolo
" ſenatoribus, conciliorum locis, novem maris
" propugnaculum, ſummo labore, vigiliâ, &
" celeritate, decretis quoque, & de ſuo perſo-
lutis

---

*a* Pieru Winſemii hiſt. de rebus Friſicis, l iii. p 251.     a Ex relat. v. Joh. de Laet.

" lutis diligentiæ præmiis, tribus plus minus
" menfibus à fundamentis erexerit, & ad fum-
" mam manum perduxerit, atque hunc lapidem,
" fublatis controverfiarum litibus terminum effe
" voluit · gratus Provincialium ordo, ob rem
" prudenter, benè & fideliter geftam, de fe ac
" de Republicâ optimè merito."

In this province, likewife, and in Groningen,
which joins to it, many lakes have likewife been
drained of late years, which are now become
moft fruitful paftures amongft which the moft
remarkable was a certain fenny tract, which in
the Dutch language they called de Wilde
Weemh· which, at the cofts of feveral merchants of Amfterdam, is become fuch rich mea-
dow ground, that within thefe fix or feven years
about the number of ten thoufand people went
thither to plant themfelves, who now live there
very happily.

## CHAP. VIII

## ZEELAND.

IN the year MDXXXV, the new haven of Mid-
dleburg, (a) in the Ifland of Walcren, paffing in a ftraight line from the town to the
bank of the Ifland, where it falls into the fea,
was finifhed Before this, then haven was near
the falt marfhes of Armuyden, having a circular
courfe into the town, and there very incon-
venient

And in the year MDXLVII, (b) Adolph of
Burgundy, fignor of Chapelle and Wackene,
Jerofme Sandelin, fignior of Herentont, receiv-
er of Bewefterfcheldt in Zeeland, and fome
private gentlemen recovered and walled in, about
Sheerenfkerke, and Henkepfandt, in the county of Zuydheveclandt, otherwife called the Ifle
of Ter Goes, the old inclofure of Poldor, which
is a land won from the fea, and which before
the inundation, was ufually called Zeefhuys,
fo that it remained a long time unprofitable,
but fince its recovery, they call it Cray, and at
this prefent time is a moft fertile country.

*a* Hift of the Netherlands, p. 161. *b.* Ibid, p. 177.

It would require a volume to give inftances
of the numberlefs works of this nature in thefe
Low countries, by banks, drains, and fluices.
Nor have they been lefs active in Brabant. (a)
for in the opinion of the learned, that country,
now a fair and dry habitation, has been fea, almoft as far as Tongerne

## CHAP. IX.

## HOLSTEIN.

IN Holfatia likewife, about Dithmarfh, and
the tracts of Wilftar, and Crempen, confift-
ing of low grounds and fubject to inundations;
Johannes Adolphus, Duke of Holftein, beginning in the year MDCX, by noble works, within
the compafs of five years, fecured many thoufand acres, and improved the lands above three
hundred thoufand dollars which being effect-
ed, he parcelled them out by gift or fale to his
fubjects, referving out of every portion, a rent
unto himfelf, " Tantum territorii fubditis &
" amicis ceffit, ea lege, ut vel aggeribus cin-
" gatur, vel ab aquis inteftinis liberetur, &
" hinc quotannis celfitudinis fuæ ærario, cer-
" tus Canon, pro quolibet (b) demeto nume-
" retur," as the learned Schoneveldeus reports.

## CHAP. X.

## AMERICA.

NEITHER do we want examples of this
nature in America, for the city of Mex-
ico, being fituate in a great lake, frequently
fubject to inundations, which had almoft deftroyed it ; in the year MDCXXXIII, the Span-
iards, with mighty induftry, fecured that habitation, by turning the lake, and fo laying the city
dry.

CHAP.

*a* Nennius Alemanenfis. *b* Every demetum contains 36
virgæ in length, and 6 in breadth, and every virga 16 feet.
In Scithyolologia. p. 47.

## CHAP. XI.

HAVING now done with my obfervations of the moft remarkable Bankings and Drainings in foreign parts, which, by way of introduction, I thought proper to take notice of, I come to England, that being the chief place of my intended difcourfe: in which, for my more orderly proceeding, I purpofe to begin with Kent, in refpect of its eaftern fitua tion; and firft, of Romney Marfh, a fpacious tract in that county, and more antiently fecured from the inundations of the ocean, than any other part of this realm, as may be obferved by the laws and conftitutions for regulating its repair, which have been long ago made the rule and ftandard, to which all the other marfhes and fens in this nation ought to conform

And in the next place, to take a view of the other furrounded marfhes in that county, as well adjacent to the Thames, as bordering on the fea: and having done this, to afcend up the ftream of that fair river, on the fouth fide. and, then defcending on the north fide, to obferve whatever I have met with memorable, in refer ence to any marfhes that lie on either. Thence into Suffex, Somerfetfhire, Gloucefterfhire Yorkfhire, and Lincolnfhire; and laftly to that great level, which extends itfelf no lefs than 60 miles, and into fix counties, viz Cambridge Huntingdon, Northampton, Norfolk, Suffolk. and Lincolnfhire, with which I fhall conclude this work.

How long fince, or by whom, this fruitful and large tract, containing no lefs than twenty-four thoufand acres, (a) was gained from the fea, there are no records left from any hiftorian, that ever I could difcover. which defect doe ftrongly prove that the firft gaining thereo was a work of much greater antiquity.

To attribute it to the Britons, the firft in habitants of this nation, or to the Saxons, who fucceeded them, I dare not advance, the firft of thefe, being a people fo rude and barbarous, that they were not verfed in any arts, and the latter fo illiterate, for the moft part, that little of invention can juftly be afcribed to them. That it was therefore a work of the Romans, whilft they were mafters here, is the opinion of fome learned men, I make no doubt of it, confidering to what a height, not only in learning, but in every art and fcience that people were arrived, as by many teftimonies we plainly find. Befides, it is not only evident, from the credit of our beft hiftorians, that their feveral colonies difperfed throughout this nation, were fo excellently difciplined; that, for avoiding the mifchiefs, which idlenefs produces, they were always exercifed in fome profitable employments, fuch as thofe great and public ways, (a) and other ftupendous works, made and raifed by their fkill and induftry, do fufficiently prove: but by the teftimony of Tacitus, an author of that time who tells us, that the Britons complained that the Romans (b) wore out and confumed their bodies, and hands, " in fylvis & " paludibus emuniendis, i. e in clearing the " woods, and banking the fens," for the word *emuniendis* muft have a fenfe, as well alluding to *paludibus* as *fylvis*.

It is true, that *munire viam* is a phrafe ufed by Cicero, for the paving a road, or making a caufey. (c) and fome are of opinion, that here, the words *paludibus emuniendis*, are to have the like fignification, and to be conftrued in making caufeys over the fens but if it fhould, as I cannot well admit, it muft be granted, that before any pavement or caufeys could be made in fuch places, the water was, of neceffity, firft to be taken and kept off, by draining and banking. fo that, allowing that conftruction, what I endeavour to prove will be fufficiently fupported, viz. that the bankings and drainings, both here and in fome other parts of this realm, which were, before that time, overflowed by fea-tides, was a work of the Romans, as when I come to Holland in Lincolnfhire, and Marfhland in Norfolk, I purpofe more fully to fhew

And therefore fince the Romans did fomething

---

a Lamb. param. of Kent (edit, Lond. 1656.) p. 211.

a Watling-ftreet, Foffee, Ermin-ftreet Ikenild, and divers others　b In vita Agricolæ.　c Dr. Holland, in his tranfla. of Cambd Brit.

thing of this kind, as will be more evident in my difcourfe of Holland and Marfhland, from undoubted teftimonies, I cannot but fuppofe, that this marfh was a part thereof, in regard, that not long after their leaving this country, I find that it was then inhabited  For in the year DCCXCVI, (a) it is thus related of Ceolf king of Mercia, viz  that " Cantiam vaftavit & pro-" vinciam quæ dicitur Merfcwari," which no doubt is meant of this Romney Marfh  for the learned Camden, in his Britannia, fays, that in the time of the Saxons, the inhabitants were called merfc war, id eft, viri paluftres, marfh-men, which agrees with the nature of this place

There are fome who fuppofe, that the name of it, viz  Romeney declares that it was, at firft won from the fea by the Romans  (b) but Mr Lambert fays it was, in the Saxons time, written Rumen-ea id eft, the large watry place  and fince it has been called Rumenale, and Romenale, agreeable to which expreffion I find, that the river, paffing through this marfh, was antiently called Rumenea  for fo it appears by that grant of Pleigmund (c) the archbifhop, made to Chrift's Church, Canterbury, about the year DCCCC, in thefe words——" Concedo " ecclefiæ Chrifti, terram quæ vocatur Wefing " merfc, juxta flumen quod vocatur Rumen-" ea "

Having now, by thefe teftimonies, fhewn, that the Romans by their fkill and experience in fuch works of banking and draining, did firft gain this rich and large tract of ground, from the impetuous fea-tides, I fhall now defcend to thofe ftatutes and ordinances, which the care and wifdom of fucceeding ages made, for the prefervation and defence of that tract, from being again drowned and deftroyed, by the violent over-flowings of the ocean

That the common laws of England, of which we find no original, were at firft certain conftitutions (d) made by fome of the antient kings and rulers of this nation, there is none I prefume can doubt, though there is no other authority to fupport them, than long ufage and cuftom.  Of the fame nature I fuppofe were thofe ftatutes and ordinances which were made for the prefervation of this marfh: for though we are yet to learn, when and by whom they were firft compofed, it is evident from the teftimony of unqueftionable records, that above four hundred years fince, they were called "antiquas " & approbatas confuetudines;" i. e. antient and approved cuftoms: (a) For, in 35 H III. the king, directing his writ to the fheriff of Kent, and thereby declaring, that complaint having been made to him, on the behalf of the xxiv jurors, made choice of for the prefervation of the marfh and fea banks of Rumenale, importing, that whereas in perfuance of their antient and approved cuftoms, they had diftrained thofe who ought of right to repair thofe banks, according to the proportion of their tenements, for the defence of all the country againft the fea  and that the faid fheriff had made replevin of the fame diftreffes; commanded him, that in cafe he had fo done, he fhould return them back to the guardians, and permit thofe jurors to ufe their cuftoms and liberties, for the defence of themfelves and others againft the fea, as they ought and had been ufed to do, left farther complaint fhould be made thereof, and that by him any damage might come to the faid king and kingdom, becaufe, as the fame mandate expreffes it, they are ready to exhibit juftice to every complainant, according to their cuftoms to that time obtained and ufed; and likewife to abide the law, as they ought and had been wont to do, if they had in any thing tranfgreffed againft thofe ufual cuftoms:  By which precept he was moreover forbidden to make any future replevin, by virtue of whatever writ from the faid king: " quia neceffitas defenfionis talis " inopinato, fi venerit, fays the record, legi " communi vel juftitiæ fubeffe non poterit " i. e  becaufe the unforefeen neceffity of fuch defence, in cafe it fhould happen, cannot be fubject to the common law, or juftice.

Nay, fo tender was the faid king, for the prefervation and fecurity of this famous and fruitful marfh, that, the year following, by his letters patent, (b) bearing date at S Edmundfbury, the fecond of September, directed like-wife

a Ethelw Chron l iii f 478. a  b Peramb of Kent, p. 208 c Lel Coll. vol. ii. p 57. d Doctor and Student, c. 7.

a 1 Clauf. 35 H. III. m. 16. in dorfo.  b Clauf. 36 H. III. 8 m.

wife to the fheriff of Kent, making this recital, *viz.* that becaufe xxiv lawful men, of the marfh of Rumenale, elected and fworn for that purpofe, time out of mind, ought to make diftreffes upon all thofe, who have lands in the faid marfh, for the repairing of the banks and water-courfes againft the violence and danger of the fea and upon all others who are obliged and bound to the repair of the faid banks and water-courfes, he granted to thofe xxiv, that for the fecurity of the faid marfh, they fhould make thofe diftreffes, fo that they were done equally, according to the proportion, more or lefs, which each man had therein, and according as fome of them were obliged and bound and therefore commanded the faid fheriff, that for avoiding of peril, he fhould neither by himfelf, nor his bailiffs, meddle with the diftreffes fo made by the appointment of the faid xxiv jurors. Farther fignifying, that whoever fhould make complaint to him on confideration of the faid diftreffes, he would do him juftice in his own court, and referve that juftice to himfelf, or his own fpecial mandate.

But after this, *viz.* in the 41 H III. (a) it being reprefented to the faid king, by certain of his loyal fubjects; whereas, time beyond memory, judgments ought to be made by xxiv lawful men of the marfh of Romenale, to that purpofe chofen and fworn, for the diftraining of all thofe who had lands in the faid marfh, to the repair of thofe banks and water-courfes, againft the force of the fea, and danger of inundation by other waters; as likewife of all thofe, who were otherwife obliged or bound to thofe repairs, he the faid king, by his fpecial mandates bearing date at Mertone the xvith of April, directed to Henry de Bathe, a famous juftice itinerant of that time, reciting his letters patent next above-mentioned, with the power thereby given to the faid xxiv jurors concerning the taking of diftreffes, as aforefaid; and fignifying, that the faid xxiv jurors having had oppofition and refiftance by certain perfons of the faid marfh, who were obliged to the repair of thofe banks and water-gangs, according to the quantity of the lands which they had therein, were not able to make the before-fpe-

cified diftreffes whereupon, the faid banks and water-gangs being not repaired, the inundations from the fea and other waters overflowed this marfh, to the ineftimable damage of the faid king, and the inhabitants thereof Being therefore defirous to provide for his own profit and indemnity, and the men of the faid marfh, he conftituted the faid Henry de Bathe, his juftice, to hear and determine the controverfies relating to thofe repairs, rifen between the faid jurors and the marfh men, who were fo obliged to the faid repairs, according to the quantity of their lands and tenements lying therein, and according to what fome men were otherwife bound or obliged, commanding him, that at a certain day and place, to be by him appointed, he fhould be in thofe parts, to hear and determine the faid controverfies, and to provide for the fecurity and defence of the faid marfh, as aforefaid And moreover to fignify in writing diftinctly and plainly, unto him the faid king, what he had done therein, that the fame might be inrolled And directed likewife his mandate to the fheriff of Kent, that at a certain day and place to be affigned by the faid Henry, he fhould caufe fuch and fo many honeft and lawful men, of this bailiwick, to come before him; by which perfons the faid differences might be the more fully determined, and provifion made for fecurity of the faid marfh. And that the faid fheriff fhould perfonally affift and attend the faid Henry therein, as he on the faid king's behalf, fhould enjoin.

By authority of which prefcript, the faid Henry de Bathe, with his affociates, viz Nicholas de Hanlou, and Alured de Dene, (a) fite at Romenhale upon the Saturday after the Feaft of the Nativity of the bleffed Virgin, in the faid xliii year of king Henry the third, before-mentioned, to which place the faid fheriff of Kent, his affiftant, by virtue likewife of the faid writ, then brought thither fo many and fuch lawful men of his bailiwick, as aforefaid, by whom thefe differences might be determined, and provifion made for the fafety of the faid marfh And the faid Henry, at the requeft of the council of the commonalty of the faid marfh, then and there likewife being, and none of the marfhmen

a Pat. 42 H III m. 10 in dorfo

a Clauf 42 H III in dorfo m 9.

men oppofing it, made and conftituted thefe following ordinances, *viz*

" 1 That twelve lawful men fhould be made " choice of, *(a)* by the commonalty of the faid " marfh, *viz.* fix of the fee of the archbifhop " of Canterbury, and fix of the barony, who " being fworn, fhould meafure both tne new " banks and the old, and thofe other, which " ought to be new made; the meafure to be, " by one and the fame perch, fcil of xx foot " And that afterwards the faid jurors fhould " likewife, according to the fame perch, mea-" fure by acres all the lands and tenements, " which were fubject to danger, within the faid " marfh All the faid meafure, being fo made, " that then xxiv men, firft elected by the com-" monalty, and fworn, having refpect to the " quantity of the banks of thofe lands, which " lay fubject to peril, upon their oaths to ap-" point every man his fhare and portion of the " faid banks, which fhould fo belong to him, " to be made and fuftained, fo that, accord-" ing to the proportion of the acres fubject to " danger, there fhould be affigned to every man " his fhare of perches, and that the faid affign-" ation fhould be made by certain limits, fo " that it might be known where, and by what " places, and how much, each man fhould be " obliged to maintain

" 2 That when neceffity fhould happen, by " occafion whereof it might be requifite to with-" ftand or refift the danger and violence of the " fea, in repairing of the before fpecified banks, " that the faid xxiv jurors fhould meet, and " view the places of danger, and confider to " whom the defence of the fame fhould be af-" figned, and within what time to be repaired.

" 3. That the common bailiff of the faid " marfh fhould give notice to thofe, to whofe " defence the faid places fhould be affigned, that " they fhould defend and repair them, within " the time affigned, by the faid xxiv jurors: " and if they neglected fo to do, that then the " faid common bailiff fhould, at his own charge, " make good the faid repairs, by the overfight " of the xxiv jurors and that afterwards, the " party fo neglecting fhould be obliged to ren-

" der to the faid bailiff, double the charge fo " laid out by him about thofe repairs, which " double to be referved for the benefit of the " faid banks, and the repair of them : and that " the party fo neglecting fhould be diftrained " for the fame, by his lands, fituate within the " faid marfh.

" 4 Moreover, in cafe any parcel of land " fhould be held in common by partners, fo that " a certain place could not be affigned to each " partner for his own proportion, *viz* a whole " or half perch, in refpect of the fmall quantity " of land; that it fhould be ordained by the " oaths of the xxiv jurors, and viewed what pro-" portion of the faid land fo held in common he " might be able to defend, and thereupon a cer-" tain portion fo to be defended by the faid " partners, in common, to be affigned to them. " And if any of the faid partners fhould neg-" lect to defend his portion, after admonition " given to them by the bailiff, the faid portion " of the party fo neglecting to be affigned to " the other partners, who ought to make the " like defence : which partners to hold the por-" tion of the party fo neglecting, in their hands, " until he fhould pay his proportion of the cofts " laid out for the faid defence, by the view of " the xxiv jurors; and alfo double towards the " fupport of the faid banks, and the repair of " them, as aforefaid.

" 5. That if all the partners fhould happen " to be negligent in the premifes ; then that the " common bailiff before-mentioned fhould make " good the whole defence, at his own proper " cofts, and afterwards diftrain all thofe part-" ners, in double the charges fo by him expend-" ed in the faid defence, by view of the xxiv " jurors as aforefaid : faving to the chief lords " in the faid marfh, the right which they have " againft their tenants, concerning this defence, " according to their feoffments.

" 6. And (laftly) that all the lands in the faid " marfh be kept and maintained againft the vio-" lence of the fea, and the floods of the frefh " waters, with banks and fewers, by the oath " and confideration of xxiv jurors at the leaft,

" for

D

*a.* The Ordinances of Henry de Bathe.

" for their preservation, as antiently had been
" accustomed. (a)

About this time I find, that the king had information that his haven of Rumenale was in great danger of destruction, to the no small damage of the public, and excessive annoyance of the town of Rumenale, unless the course of the river of Newendene, on which the said haven was founded, being then diverted by the overflowings of the sea, were reduced to the said port: and that he was informed by an inquisition, made by Nicholas de Handlon, whom he had sent into those parts, to provide and ordain in what sort the said stream might be again brought back to the same haven, by its antient channel, or a new one made; that it could not be so reduced, nor the said haven preserved for the common benefit of the said port and town, except certain obstructions, which were in the old course of that river, were removed, and that a new channel were made, near to the same old course, viz. from a certain cross, belonging to the hospital of infirm people at Rumenale, standing by Aghenepend, to Effetone, and from Effetone to the house of William de Byll, and so to Melepend, and thence descending to the said port, so that a sluice be made under the town of Apeltre, for reception of the salt-water entering into the said river, by the inundation of the sea, from the parts of Winchelsea, and for retaining the same in its passage and return to the sea, to the intent that the same water might come, together with the fresh water of that river, by the antient course into the before specified new course; and so by that passage directly to descend and fall into the said haven. And that another sluice should be made at Sneregate; and a third near the said port, where that water might descend into the sea, for restraint only of the sea-tide on that part, that it enter not into the said course, but reserving the antient and oblique course from the said cross to the before mentioned haven.

The king, therefore, providently desiring the common benefit and safe-guard of the said port, by this precept, dated at Oxford, the xxift of June, commanded the said Nicholas, that he should repair in his person, on a certain day assigned, to those parts; together with the sheriff of Kent, to whom the said king had sent his writ; and by the oaths of xxiv as well knights, as other free and lawful men of the neighbourhood, by whom the truth might be the better known, to make estimation how much of other mens lands would be necessary to be taken, for the making of the said new channel and sluices, and what those lands were worth by the year; and to make speedy assignation to the tenants of those lands, to the value of the same lands or more, out of the lands, or money of the barons and honest men of the said port, as also to remove the said obstructions in the old channel, and to make the said new channel and sluices, in the lands of whomever it should be requisite, for the common benefit and advantage of the said port and town of Rumenale, as aforesaid. And the said sheriff of Kent was likewise commanded, that he should diligently assist and attend the before mentioned Nicholas, in this business, and to cause the said xxiv knights and others of the neighbourhood, as aforesaid, to be before the said Nicholas, at the same day and place.

But, notwithstanding these ordinances, so made by the said Henry de Bathe, for the defence and preservation of this marsh, and taking distresses for that purpose, and also, notwithstanding the former precepts from the king to the sheriff of Kent, forbidding him to intermeddle at all with any more distresses, so taken as I have at large already shewn, it appears that the sheriff did again make replevin of some distresses, taken by virtue of those ordinances (a) for in 43 H. III. I find, that the king issued out another writ to the said sheriff, bearing date the xxth of April, requiring him to return back those distresses, to the end no more complaint might be made against him upon that occasion, for which he might further incur the said king's displeasure.

To give instance of all the particular persons who opposed these ordinances, it would be too tedious, could it exactly be done. I shall therefore take notice of one only suit in this case, which

---

a Pat 42 H III m 7.

a Ex cod. MS penes Oliv, S John Arm f 9 a.

which was commenced by one Godfrey le Fauconer, against Hamon Pitte, John Cobbe, and others, for taking ten cows by way of distress, upon his the said Godfrey's manor of Hurst, for his disobedience to the said ordinances to which action the said Hamon and his fellow defendants pleaded, that the said Godfrey enjoyed certain possessions, lying in Romney Marsh, in which marsh, all who hold any lands, ought, according to the quantity of their tenements, to make the banks and water courses, against the sea, and other inundations of water, and that the xxiv men of the marsh, chosen and sworn by the commonalty thereof, ought to make distresses in the same, upon all the landholders, according to the quantity of their tenements, whenever the banks and water courses should stand in need of repair Which said jurors as the custom was, because they could not attend to it themselves, made choice of the said Hamon to take those distresses, and constituted him their bailiff so to do and that they have this liberty by the antient custom of the said marsh, and by the king's charter, which they then produced.

Whereupon they say, that, by reason of the said Godfrey's default, that distress taken for repair of those banks and water-gangs was justly made of which, there were assigned by the said juries, three perch and a half at the least, for his proportion in the bank of Apuldre, to be repaired at his cost, and according to the overflowing of the waters, more if need should be, in different places and whether they might not have taken a greater distress upon him, they appeal to the country

They say nevertheless that they took upon one A. B. a farmer to the said Godfrey, ten steers and ten lambs, belonging to J N tenant also to the said Godfrey, by reason of his default in repairing the said banks and water-gangs, for which they afterwards made satisfaction, and had their cattle again And being questioned for how much he took the first distress, and for how much the second; he said, that the first default of the said Godfrey was estimated at four marks, and the second at xlviii shillings

And the said Godfrey alleged, that he held those tenements in the marsh aforesaid, by the grant of Henry some time king of England, grand-father to king Henry then being . and that the said king Henry gave them to William the son of Balderic, ancestor of the said Godfrey, whose heir he is and that by this grant, both his ancestors and himself after them, always held their tenements in the said marsh, as freely and quietly as the said Balderic first held them And he farther said, that this custom for the repair of those banks and water-gangs, was never required, neither of these said ancestors nor himself, till about five years then last past, that the said Hamon was made bailiff for the custody of the same banks and water-gangs ; nor that they ever made them at any time ; and produced the charter of the said king Henry the second . and moreover said, that his ancestors held those tenements, by that feoffment, so freely that they never did any repair to the said banks nor water-gangs . and that neither he, after he was possessed of the said lands, nor his ancestors, were distrained, till within these five or six years last past, that the said Hamon, and others took his cattle , and forasmuch as they knew who they were that made those distresses, for that defect in repairing the said banks and water-gangs, which neither he nor his ancestors made, nor were used to make , he required judgment of their recognition

Whereunto the said Hamon and the rest replied, that in former time, there was a difference betwixt the tenants in the said marsh, concerning the repair of the before-mentioned banks and water-gangs , upon which there arose a suit in the country before the sheriff, wherein the said xxiv jurors thinking themselves wronged, came to the king's court, and complained to the sheriff, alleging this plea did not belong to the sheriff, to hold · It was therefore determined by the king's council, that the king's justices should be sent thither, to order and settle those differences , and accordingly, Henry de Bathe being sent, all the tenants of the said marsh had summons of xl days, as in the *Iter* of the justices ; and the said Henry, upon his view of those banks and water-gangs, by the consent and approbation

tion of the whole commonalty of the said marsh, then ordained, that the archbishops, bishops, priors, earls, barons, and all the tenants in the said marsh, should contribute to the repair of those banks and water-gangs, according to the quantity of their tenements. Upon which, as the said Godfrey desired to be defended by the said banks and water-gangs, the said Hamon required, that he the said Godfrey should contribute to those repairs, as it was ordained in the presence of the said justice. and that there was such an ordinance as aforesaid, he referred himself to the record, in the rolls of the said Henry de Bathe.

And also the said Hamon farther alleged, that of necessity the said Godfrey ought to contribute to the said bank, &c because, that if his land should not be defended by them, it would be wholly drowned and made salt. But to this the said Godfrey answered, that though that ordinance was so made by the said Henry, yet he the said Godfrey never gave his consent thereto; and that he was neither summoned, nor called to come before him at the making thereof And moreover affirmed that neither before the said ordinance, so made, nor after, either he or his ancestors ever so contributed; but always held their land quietly without any exaction at all, according to the tenor of the before-mentioned king Henry's charter, grandfather to the present king Henry, until two years before that the said Hamon and others took his cattle, whereupon he required judgement, whether the same ordinance ought to prejudice him in that behalf.

To which the said Hamon and others replied, that he had the common summons of xl days, in such sort as the whole commonalty of the said marsh had, of which he ought not to be ignorant; and thereupon said, that though the said Godfrey would not come, as he ought to have done, with his neighbours, he ought not therefore to be free from payment of the before-mentioned contribution, for repair of those banks, because it conduced to the common advantage of all the tenants in the said marsh; that as well his lands, as the lands of the other tenants, were

defended by the said banks and water-gangs; whereupon he required judgement. And he also alleged, that after the said ordinance, the said Godfrey and his tenants gave one mark towards the repair of the said banks and water-gangs, before he the said Hamon was bailiff, and that this he was ready to justify

To which the said Godfrey answered, that he held himself to the before-mentioned charter of king Henry, and to the liberty, which he and his ancestors had enjoyed; against which no ordinance, made by the said Henry de Bathe, could or ought to do him prejudice, and stood upon it, that neither himself, nor any by him, had given aught, either before the said ordinance so made, or afterwards; and that this he was ready to justify.

After which, on the morrow after the feast of St Martin, in the xlii of H. III came to the said Godfrey, Hamon, and others, and the sheriff had command, that he should bring xii, as well knights, as others, having no lands in the said marsh, on the morrow three weeks after Easter, by whom the truth might be the better discovered, to inquire, whether the said Godfrey and his ancestors, after they had their land of Hurst, of the gift and grant of the before-mentioned king Henry, had wont to repair the said banks and water-gangs, together with others that had lands in the said marsh, and to contribute with them for their repair, when need should require Upon which the said Godfrey, by a certain ordinance, in which he acknowledged before the said Henry de Bathe, whom the king had sent to that purpose, that though he gave a mark to the repair of the said banks and water-gangs, before the said Hamon was bailiff of the said marsh, as they the said Hamon and John did affirm; yet he appealed, whether himself or his ancestors were not quit of the said repairs, and payments thereto by the charter of king Henry, grandfather to the present king, forasmuch as he did not consent to the said ordinance, nor ever gave any thing to the repair of those banks and water-gangs, as he affirmed.

But the sheriff, not making his prescript as above-

above-faid, was amerced, and another writ directed to him, to fummon the faid xii men, to appear, &c. the morning after the feaft of the holy Trinity; at which time the faid Godfrey, Hamon, and others, came, and required, that judgement fhould be given according to the record and procefs upon the before-mentioned plea Whereupon the plea was recited before the king and his council, and becaufe it was found, according to that record, that the king had fent Henry de Bathe, his juftice with full powers unto the faid marfh of Romenale, who determined, that all they who had lands in the faid marfh ought to contribute, according to the proportion of their tenements, for the repair of the faid banks and water-gangs thereof, as the faid Hamon and others did allege, and to which contribution he the faid Godfrey affirmed he was not obliged, and that as yet nothing did appear to the king's court here, of the faid ordinance or determination, without which of right, there could be no proceeding to judgement, a farther day was given, viz. until the xvme of S Michael, that in the mean time, the rolls of the faid Henry de Bathe might be looked into, and that the plea thus depending, no diftrefs fhould be further made upon the faid Godfrey.

At which time, viz in the xvme of S. Michael, in the 43 H III the faid Godfrey came, and withdrew his procefs againft the faid Hamon and others, therefore, being amerced, he confented for himfelf and his heirs, that for the future they would repair the faid banks and water-gangs, together with their neighbours, according to the quantity of their land, as it was the cuftom of that country, without any conteft, or contradiction whatever,

And that the faid Hamon granted and became obliged, for himfelf and the reft, that he would make a due account, before the xxiv jurors, chofen by the country, concerning the diftrefles and chattels of the faid Godfrey, taken from the time of the beginning of the fuit, until that prefent and deducting fo much, as fhould be fufficient to fatisfy the faid repairs, according to the proportion, belonging to the faid Godfrey, to repay the furplufage of the money, for the chattels of him the faid Godfrey fo fold and

the faid Godfrey agreed, that if the faid Hamon, by his account could make it manifeft, that the value of the chattels fo diftrained by him for the caufe premifed, would not fuffice for his portion, in repair of the faid banks and water-gangs, according to the quantity of his lands, he the faid Godfrey would make fatisfaction to him of the whole arrearage, from the beginning of the fuit, till that prefent time, according to the view and eftimation of the before xxiv jurors of the county.

The next thing memorable relating to this marfh, is, that king Edward the firft, by his letters patent, (a) bearing date at Weftminfter, the xxth of Novem. in the xvith year of his reign, granted a commiffion to John de Lovetot, and Henry de Apuldrefeld, to view the banks and drains upon the fea-coaft and parts adjacent, within the county of Kent, in many places then broken, through the violence of the fea, and to inquire by whofe default this damage had happened, and, together with the bailiffs of liberties, and others in thofe parts, to diftrain all thofe, which held any lands and tenements there, and had or might have defence and prefervation, in any fort, by the faid banks and drains, according to the quantity of their faid lands and tenements, either by the number of acres, or by carucates, for the proportion of what they held, for the neceffary repair of thofe banks and drains, and as often, and where there fhould be need; fo that no man, of what condition, ftate, or dignity foever, who had fafeguard in any fort by thofe walls or banks, whether it were within liberties or without, fhould have favour therein commanding alfo the faid John and Henry, to behave themfelves fo faithfully and difcretely, in the execution of this bufinefs, that as well the men refiding in thofe parts, as their lands, fhould be fafe againft the like dangers, or perhaps worfe, no cuftom favourably introduced, notwithftanding, and that of their transaction in this employment, they fhould diftinctly and plainly certify the faid king, under their feals, and the feals of the jurors as well knights, as other honeft and lawful men commanding, moreover, his fheriff of Kent, to caufe fo many and fuch perfons of his bailiwick, to appear before

a Ex præfato cod MS f xi. a.

fore the said John and Henry, at certain days and places, of which he should give them notice, by whom the truth in the premises might be the better inquired into, and known.

By virtue of which mandate, the said sheriff was required to summon the xxiv jurors of the marsh of Rumenal, and all the lords of the banks of the said marsh, as also such and so many honest and lawful men, of all the maritime lands in his bailiwick, by whom the truth in the premises might be the better inquired into, and known, and to do farther in the premises, as it should then and there be decreed. Who came accordingly. And the said xxiv jurors of the marsh before named, together with the commonalty of the said marsh, affirmed, that King Henry, father of the present king, did by his charter grant to them certain liberties, in his own lands, within the said marsh. and they therefore required, that those their liberties might be preserved, and also that nothing might be attempted, or decreed in prejudice of their said liberties, and produced the said charter of King Henry

They likewise alleged, that King Henry, father to the present king, in the xlii year of his reign, by reason of a certain controversy, arisen betwixt divers men of this marsh, occasioned for the repair of the banks and water-gangs therein, sent Henry de Bathe, his justice, into those parts, to hear and determine the differences in that business, between the xxiv jurors and the same marsh-men, and to provide for the defence and security thereof, and against the peril of inundation by other waters, in causing the banks and water-gangs to be repaired, by those who were obliged thereto, for the lands which they held therein, according to the proportion thereof. Whereupon they affirmed that the said Henry de Bathe, by authority of the said King Henry's mandate, ordered and decreed for them a certain law and ordinance; by which this marsh was to that time kept and preserved; and therefore desired, that they might for the future, be guided and defended by that ordinance and law, as they had been accustomed till that present time. and thereupon produced the said ordinances of him the said Henry, under the king's seal.

1 Because the said ordinance seemed consonant to equity, (a) and had been to that time approved, command was given, and it was decreed, that the same should be in all things observed, without diminution, adding nevertheless, that in regard there was no mention therein of the election of the king's common bailiff in the said marsh, how and by whom he ought to be chosen, it was determined, that for the future, upon the decease of the said common bailiff, or his quitting the office, another to be chosen, who shall reside, and have lands in this marsh. and that the said election should thenceforth be, by the common assent of the lords of the towns lying therein, or by their attornies, and as the major part should determine, to submit to that election; because till that time the custom had been so

2. And concerning that double of the costs, imposed for repairing the defaults, to be levied upon those, through whose neglect they had happened, it was decreed, that the same double should be levied in such sort, as by the former ordinance had been appointed, and employed to the common profit of this marsh, and not to the behalf of the said bailiff.

3. Forasmuch as there were several banks and water-gangs in the said marsh, to the maintenance of which the commonalty thereof did not contribute, except only those whose lands lay contiguous to the said banks and water-gangs, and that some, through the oppression of the lords of the said marsh, did sometime pay as much for the repair and maintenance of those banks and water-gangs, for forty acres, as others did for fifty, which was much against the law of the marsh, and the ordinance of the said Henry de Bathe: it was therefore decreed and ordained, that notwithstanding any custom, by whomever introduced; all and singular persons, who had lands therein, which were subject to the danger of the sea, and had preservation by the said banks and water-gangs, should thenceforth be distrained for the reparation and maintenance of them; (b) so that every man might contribute

---

*a* The ordinances of John de Lovetot, and Henry de Apuldrefeld  Election of the common bailiff  *b* That contribution for the repair of the banks be equal, according to the number of acres

contribute equally, according to the number of acres which he poſſeſſed therein, and that no perſon, of whatever ſtate or condition, who had preſervation and defence thereby, ſhould be favoured.

4. Before that time, in this marſh of Romenale, beyond the courſe of the water of that port, running from Suergate, towards Romenale, on the weſt part of the ſame port, till it come to the county of Suſſex, there had not been any certain law of the marſh, ordained nor uſed, otherwiſe than at the will of thoſe who had lands in the ſame, inſomuch as many dangers and intolerable loſſes happened by the ſea's inundation to the end therefore, that the like perils might in future be prevented, and the common benefit provided for, it was agreed and jointly ordained, that in the ſaid marſh, beyond the before-mentioned port, towards Suſſex, (a) there ſhould be jurors eſtabliſhed, choſen by the commonalty, who being ſworn to that purpoſe, for the ſecurity of thoſe parts, having reſpect to the number of acres, ſubject to that danger, and to the proportion of the banks and watergangs, to be repaired and maintained there, ſhould, on their oaths, conſider and ordain how much might be neceſſary for ſuch repair, ſo that according to the proportion of their acres, and value of them, there might be aſſigned in the ſaid banks and water-gangs, an equal portion of acres, to be maintained, as is more fully contained in the ordinance of the ſaid Henry de Bathe.

5. And moreover, foraſmuch as there had been no common bailiff conſtituted in thoſe parts, beyond the before mentioned port, towards Suſſex, who ought, for the public benefit, take care and provide againſt the damages there happening, and to prevent the like in future, it was ordained, that there ſhould be one common bailiff choſen in the ſaid marſhes, beyond that courſe of the water toward Suſſex, for overſeeing, keeping, and repairing the ſaid banks and water-gangs, in ſuch places and bounds of the ſaid whole marſh, as ſhould ſeem moſt expedient to all the commonalty. as alſo to ſummon together to proper places the jurors of the ſaid marſh, as often as ſhould be required, for the making of ordinances and laws, for preſervation of the lands in thoſe parts, cauſing diſtreſſes to be made, and levying a double proportion, upon ſuch as ſhould make default; according to the tenor of the ordinance made by the ſaid Henry de Bathe Provided, that at the election of the ſaid bailiff, whenever it might happen, the lords of the towns in the ſaid marſh, beyond the ſaid courſe of the water, towards Suſſex, ſhould be ſummoned and called, if they would be preſent, as alſo the jurors and whole commonalty of that marſh

6 It was likewiſe ordained, (a) that in future the king's ſaid common bailiff in the marſh of Romenale, ſhould be the ſuperviſor of the before-mentioned bailiffs and jurors in this marſh, beyond the courſe of the water towards Suſſex, and that he ſhould ſummon together, to convenient places, all the jurors choſen on both ſides the ſaid courſe of that water, when need required, to make their ordinances and laws for preſervation of the ſaid marſhes, ſo that always, on both parts of that water-courſe, they ſhould abide by the ordinances and conſiderations of the ſaid jurors, as to the prejudice or greater ſecurity of any man's land, notwithſtanding any cuſtom whatever living always the tenor of the king's charter, granted to the commonalty of Romney marſh, and the ordinance of Henry de Bathe, ever to remain in full power and ſtrength

Not long after this, there happened certain differences, (b) between the maſter of the hoſpital, called God's Houſe, in Dover, and certain of his tenants, within the manors of Hunychild, and Eſtbrigge, in Romenale marſh, concerning ſome banks and water-gangs upon the ſea coaſt, which the ſaid maſter alleged, that his ſaid tenants for the antient demeſnes belonging to him in thoſe manors, as often as need required,

a That it might be eſtabliſhed in that part of the marſh towards Suſſex, as alſo a common bailiff of which bailiff and jurors the king's common bailiff to be ſuperviſor  b. Pat 18 E 1 m. 6, in dorſo.

required, fhould at their proper cofts repair and maintain, againft the violence of the fea, and inundations of the fiefh waters for the hearing and determining of which controverfies, according to the law and cuftom of the faid marfh, John de Lovet, Robert de Septvaus, mafter Thomas de Gudinton, and Henry de Appletrefeld, were by the king affigned Whereupon the parties in difpute, weighing all circumftances concerning the fame, put themfelves upon the inquifition of the country, but the taking thereof, in regard that the faid mafter refufed, that any perfons, refiding in the faid marfh, fhould be admitted, and the faid tenants, not being content with any foreigners, was delayed, to the great damage of thofe parts, as by complaint the king was informed to put therefore a fpeedy end to their difference, the faid king, by his letters patent, dated at Tydefwell, xxivth Sept. conftituted Stephen de Penceftre, conftable of Dover-Caftle, Henry de Appletrefeld, and Bertram de Tancrey, his juftices, to make farther inquiry but what was done therein, I have not yet learnt

About four years after, the faid king Edward (a) the firft, taking great care for the defence and prefervation of this marfh by his letters patent, bearing date at Weftminfter, xxth April, in the xviiith year of his reign, has this remarkable expreffion, viz "quod cum nos, "ratione dignitatis regiæ, & per juramentum "aftricti fumus, ad providendum falvationi "regni noftri circumquaque, i. e in refpect of "his royal dignity, and that he was obliged by "oath to provide for the fafeguard of his king- "dom on every part," affigned H. de Apeltrefeld, and Bertram de Tancrey, to overfee the banks and drains upon the fea coafts and parts adjacent, in the county of Kent, which by reafon of the roughnefs of the fea, were in many places broken; and to inquire by whofe default that damage had occurred. as alfo of all thofe who held lands and tenements in thofe parts, and had or might have protection and defence any manner of way, by the faid banks and drains, and to diftrain them for the quantity of their faid lands, or number of acres, or

carucates, according to the portion they held; together with the bailiffs of liberties, and others of thofe parts, for the repair of the faid banks and drains, in proper places, as often and where there fhould be occafion, fo that no land holder, rich or poor, of what eftate, dignity or condition foever he was, in cafe he had defence and prefervation any manner of way, by the faid banks and drains, were he within liberties or without, fhould have favour in any kind

Commanding them, moreover, that in the execution of that office they fhould behave themfelves with fuch fidelity and difcretion, that as well the inhabitants of thofe places, as their lands, might be preferved from the like dangers, and cafually worfe, any cuftom through favour, by whomever it had been introduced, notwithftanding And what they fhould do and ordain therein, to certify the faid king thereof, under their feals, and the feals of xxiv as well knights as other honeft and lawful men, diftinctly and plainly. And for their better accomplifhment of that end, directed his precept to the fheriff of Kent, appointing him, that at certain days and places, of which he was to give them proper notice, he fhould caufe to come, before the faid king's juftices, fuch and fo many honeft and lawful men of his bailiwic, by whom the truth in the premifes might be the better known and inquired into.

By virtue alfo of which mandate, the faid fheriff had command to bring before the faid juftices at that time, the xxiv jurors of Romene marfh, and all the lords of the towns therein, and fuch and fo many honeft men, of the maritime parts in his bailiwic, by whom the truth in the premifes might likewife be the better known, and inquired into; and to do farther what fhould be ordained in the premifes.

Which commiffioners came accordingly, as alfo the faid xxiv jurors, together with the commonalty of this marfh; and alleged, that king Henry, father of the faid king Edward, by his charter granted to them certain liberties in their lands within the faid marfh, and required, that thofe their liberties might be preferved, and nothing accepted or ordained in prejudice of them;

pro-

---

a Ex vet. cod MS, ad Abb. S. Aug. Cantuar. quondam fpectante, tunc veró penès Rog. Twyfden Baronettum.

ducing the charter of the said king Henry; in which was recorded the ordinance of Henry de Bathe. And, farther, declared their approbation of the said ordinance, with the additions, in such manner and form, as they had before done in the xvith year of this king's reign, before John de Lovetot and the said Henry de Apeldrefeld, then the king's justices, as I have at large already shewn, to which, for avoiding repetition, I refer my reader. Adding moreover, by common agreement, to those wholesome ordinances, these ensuing constitutions, *viz.*

" 1 That through all other maritime places " in the said county, liable to the danger of the " sea, the river of Thames, or any other water, " wherein the marsh law had not formerly been " established and used, and that many perils " through defect of banks and water-gangs had " there happened: left therefore, in future, the " like or wofre might accrue

" 2. That in every hundred and town, as " well by the sea-coast, as bordering on the " Thames and other waters, in which the marsh " lands are subject to inundation, there be " chosen and sworn xii or vi lawful men, ac- " cording to the largeness of the hundreds or " towns, and who have lands in danger of the " sea, the Thames, and other waters which " men to be assigned keepers of the banks and " water-gangs, in the hundreds and towns afore- " said, who upon their oath shall keep safe the " said banks and water-gangs; and when and " as often as need may require, repair them as " also shall, in respect of the raging of the sea, " raise the said banks higher, by four feet, at " least, than formerly they were, and make " them of thickness answerable to that height

" 3. For the repairing of which banks and " water-gangs, when need shall require the charge " to be raised in manner following; *viz.* That " all and singular persons, having lands liable " to the danger, whether situate near, or far off, " forasmuch as they have preservation by those " banks and water gangs, they shall contribute " for the quantity of their lands and tenements, " either by number of acres or carucates, ac-

" cording to the proportion of what they hold; " so that no tenant of these lands or tenements, " be he rich or poor; or of what order, state, " dignity, or condition foever, either within " liberties or without, any favour shall be shewn " in this respect.

" 4 That in every place, for the levying of " the said costs and charges, and faithfully lay- ' ing it out upon the said banks and water- " gangs, two lawful persons, out of the said " sworn men to be assigned, who, together with " the bailiffs of the liberties, or lords of the " fee, shall make distresses for the same.

"5 When the before-mentioned banks shall be " according to the ordinance of the jury, so re- " paired at the common charges, that there " shall be assigned to every man, his peculiar " portion of the bank, by certain places and " bounds, to be sustained at his own proper " costs, according to the quantity of his tene- " ment and number of acres subject to that dan- " ger, so that it may be known where, and by " what places, and to what portion, every man " is so obliged to make defence.

" 6 If any shall be negligent in paying their " portions of the said contribution, at the day " appointed by the jurors for that purpose; or " in his portion for repair of the banks, that " he be distrained by his goods and chattels, " wherever they should be found, within li- " berties or without, till he shall have contri- " buted his share, and paid his charge of the " said banks, with double costs : which double " to be reserved for the common benefit of the " like repairs in those parts.

" 7. That those distresses shall be made by " the collectors of the said costs, together with " the bailiffs of the liberties, or lords of the fee : " and, being so made, to be kept for the space " of three days at the most; if they, upon whom " they shall be made, be stubborn or negligent " for so long time, and then forthwith sold, in re- " spect of the perilous rage of the sea, imminent.

" 8. If as well the collectors, as tenants, shall " be found negligent in performing the premi- " ses, that then every lord of the fee, within " the compass of his fee, shall cause the said

E                                         banks

*a.* The ordinances of Henry de Apeldrefeld, and Bertram de Tancrey.

" banks and water-gangs to be repaired, at his
" own proper charge ; and the cofts that he fhall
" be at, together with the double thereof, he
" fhall caufe to be levied upon the goods and
" chattels of thofe who are negligent, for his
" own ufe.

" 9. That no fheriff of Kent, for the time
" being, or his bailiff or officer, fhall take any
" diftrefs, concerning the banks and water-
" gangs in any marfhes, nor thenceforth med-
" dle at all, either with the diftreffes taken by
" the lords of the fees, bailiffs of liberties, or
" collectors of the cofts or contributions to the
" faid banks and water gangs, nor diftrain them
" by writ of replevin, nor deliver them by
" furety, or pledge any manner of way.

" 10. It was alfo ordained and concluded,
" that if the jurors, fo chofen for the prefer-
" vation of the banks and water-gangs, whether
" they fhall be of this marfh of Romenale, or
" of other maritime lands, do refufe to come
" at the fummons of their bailiffs, for the pro-
" per repair of the faid banks and water-gangs,
" they fhall, for their negligence, be punifhed
" by their bailiffs, as in this marfh of Rome-
" nale, they had been accuftomed.

" 11. That the collectors alfo of the cofts,
" beftowed in repair and fupport of the banks
" and water-gangs, after the faid repairs are per-
" fected, fhall forthwith make their account,
" before the jurors and bailiff of that country,
" as well within the marfh of Romenale, as
" without, of all monies affeffed and levied for
" the before-mentioned repairs ; as alfo for
" the double, whenever it may happen to be
" levied : and if they fhall not fo do, then to
" be diftrained by the bailiffs of the country
" or place, to make account thereupon : faving
" always to the chief lords of the fees, their
" right, which they have, and hitherto ufed to
" have, concerning the defence of their lands,
" according to their feoffments, and of levying
" the double, according to antient cuftom ufed,
" as it is contained in the ordinance of the faid
" Henry de Bathe."

In teftimony whereof, Sir Walter de Ripple,
and Sir William de Haute, knights, Adam
Waftechar, William Waftechar, William le Ros,
Guy de Trulegh, John Amfrey, Peter de Ma-
ryns, Thomas le Reade, Thomas Elys, Hugh
de Suthlonde, Richard Jon, William Collol,
Henry de Bettefangre, Jordon Collol, John atte
Ware, Hamon atte Porte, John Sprott, Jacob
de Paftre, John de Moffedeime, Henry Kenet,
Thomas de Freneffe, Henry Woodman, and
William de Mereworth, have put to their feals.

That the ordinance of the faid Henry de
Bathe, for preferving this marfh was held in no
fmall efteem, we fee, by all thofe of the country, whom it immediately concerned, and it was
held likewife in high regard with the fucceeding kings of this realm, as by their confirmations of which I fhall in due place take notice
will appear. The firft of which confirmations
was made by king Edward the fecond, whofe
charter, (a) for that purpofe bears date at Weftminfter the xxiid of November, 7 E. II. In
which he firft makes mention of his grand-father
king Henry the third's patent in 36° of his
reign, by which he declares his loyal pleafure,
that no fheriff of Kent fhall intermeddle with
fuch diftreffes, as fhould be taken for the repair of the banks and water-gangs of this marfh.
And next in that of 42° which expreffes the occafion of his fending Henry de Bathe, his juftice,
into thofe parts, and at large recites the faid
ordinance then made by the faid Henry. And
then concludes thus, " Nos attendentes, quod
" impetus maris in partibus illis, plus folito
" jam accrevit, &c. i. e. " We therefore, taking
" into confideration, that the violence of the
" fea in thofe parts is grown greater than ufual ;
" by reafon of which it is neceffary that a more
" diligent care fhould be taken for the repair-
" ing of the faid banks forafmuch as by a
" breach in them, though but fmall, fhould it
" happen (as God forbid) an ineftimable and
" irrecoverable lofs muft needs accrue to us, and
" the inhabitants of the faid marfh. Purpofing
" therefore to prevent fuch damage and peril,
" and to provide for the fafety of thofe parts, as
" well for our own benefit, as the convenience
" of the faid marfh-men we do, for us and our
" heirs, as much as in us lies, ratify and con-
" firm all and fingular the things in the faid let-
" ters patent of our faid grand-father, and the
" before-

_a_ Pat. 7 E. II p. 2 m. 26.

" before mentioned ordinance contained · will-
" ing and commanding, that no sheriff of Kent,
" or any of his bailiffs, for the time being, shall
" of himself intermeddle with such distresses,
" as are, or shall be made by the direction of the
" said xxiv jurors. but that such justice as is
" to be executed thereupon, shall be reserved
" to us and our heirs, or to our special mandate,
" as it is before expressed in that patent of our
" said grand-father "

Which king, continuing his attention, by his
letters patent, (a) bearing date at York, 24° Au-
gust, in the tenth year of his reign, appointed
Robert de Kendale, John Malemeyns de Hoo,
and William de Cotes, gentlemen, to oversee the
banks in this marsh, situate between Apeldre
and Romenale

The year following, there having been a complaint made to the king, that by reason of a certain drain made betwixt Apeldre and the port
of Romenale, many inconveniences and losses
daily befel the country adjacent. (b) whereupon he assigned the before named Edmund and
John, together with William de Cotes, to inquire by the oaths of honest and lawful men of
those parts, by whom the truth in the premises
might be the better discovered, who made that
drain, and when, and for what cause; as also
how, and in what manner  and moreover, what
inconvenience and damage had occurred by
means thereof, and to whom, and in what sort
But being afterwards informed, that there was
so great a dissention risen, between his Barons of
the Cinque Ports, and the commonalty of Ro-
men Ile Marsh, that both sides were preparing
for blows, if there should be any farther proceeding in that inquisition, which, as it would occasion much terror to the people thereabouts, so
might it not a little hinder that warlike expe-
dition, which the said king then intended  Considering therefore the need that at present he had,
of the service of his faithful subjects, as well by
land, as by sea; and being desirous to his
utmost power, to provide for their unity and
peace, by his special precept, bearing date at
Guildford 6 Aug  he commanded the before-
mentioned Edmund, John and William, for the

causes above expressed, to supersede the taking
of that intended inquisition, until they should
receive his farther commands.   Which stop last-
ed not long. for in the beginning of February,
the king granted a new commission.

Greater care and regard could not have been
taken, in the regulation of all things, tending
to the safety of this marsh, than what we have
already seen · nevertheless, such is the depra-
vity of some ill-disposed men, who chiefly mind
their particular gain, though it be by cheating
the public; that were it not for a strict watch
over them, all good order would have been sub-
verted, and little else but fraud if not rapine,
practised, as we shall find by the actions of some,
who were employed with levying and collecting
monies, for the repair of those banks and water-
gangs  who, most unconscionably, and against
the trust reposed in them, made use of those
sums, so gathered, to their own private uses;
insomuch that complaint was made to the king
in 5 E. III  (a) who gave commission to William de Clinton, Ralph Sauvage, and Thomas
de Feversham, to inquire into the particulars.

Which king, out of the like tender respect
to the preservation of this marsh, as his father,
and other his ancestors had shewn, granted his letters patent, (b) bearing date at Westminster, 28°
of Nov. in the seventh year of his reign, in which
he recited that famous ordinance, made by Henry
de Bathe, of which I have so often made mention,
adding his royal confirmation: and afterwards
at different times, as occasion required, granted
his commission to several persons of quality in
the said county of Kent, for overseeing the said
banks and water-gangs, and taking care for their
support; as by the enrolments of them appears.

But notwithstanding that wholesome ordinance, so often mentioned, and the several confirmations of it, I find, that Simon Islip, archbishop of Canterbury, with other land-holders
in this marsh of Romene, made grievous complaint to the king in 33 E. III. (c) that whereas
those their lands lay bordering on the sea coast,
and without the continual support of the banks,
channels, drains, and other mounds, as well for
excluding the sea, as for conveying the fresh
E 2                                       waters,

---

a Pat. 10 E. II p. 1. m. 23. in dorso.  b. Clauf. 18 E. II.
m. 38.

a Pat. 5 E III p 2 m dorso m  19  b Pat 14 R. II p.
2 m 18  per Inspex.   c Ex cod. MS. penes Oliv. S John
Arm. f. 12. b.

waters, there made, they could not by any means be defended and preserved. Farther shewing, that for the safety thereof, it was in the time of King Henry, ancestor to the said King Edward III. ordained by Henry de Bathe, and his associates, justices of the said king, for that purpose · that every tenant and resident within that precinct, whom the greater part of the lords of the towns therein situate should chuse, ought to be the bailiff to levy the taxes, assessed for repairing and maintaining the said banks, as in the said ordinance more fully does appear. And, that though in pursuance of those ordinances, one John atte Luse, a tenant and resident within the said marsh, had been elected and deputed to the office of the said bailiff, for levying the said taxes, by the lords of this marsh, in form aforesaid : nevertheless one Matthew at More, and other his accomplices, having confederated themselves together by false contrivance, to constitute another bailiff there, in favour to his friends, and to lay a burden unjustly upon others, contrary to the before-mentioned ordinance ; did so terrify the said John, by grievous threats, and otherwise hinder him, that he neither could nr durst take upon him that office, according to the said ordinance ; so that by reason of the said bailiff's default, all the before-mentioned marsh, being daily liable to be overflown, was in danger to be destroyed, without speedy remedy obtained.

The said king therefore, taking this complaint into mature consideration ; for prevention of that imminent mischief, granted his royal commission, (a) bearing date at Westminster, 17ᵒ Febr. in the said thirty-fifth year of his reign, to Thomas de Lodelowe, Robert Belknap, and Thomas Colepepir ; appointing them, or any three or two of them, as well to oversee the said banks, drains, &c. and cause them to be repaired, as to take a view of the said ordinances : and in case they should find them any way defective, as to the defence of the said marsh, against those inundations, then to repair and amend them, and, if need were, to make a new ordinance, to direct how the said marsh might be better defended and preserved against the said waters, upon any accident that should at any time hap

pen : and to decree certain strict punishments against all those, who should transgress the said ordinances so to be made by them the said Thomas, Robert, and Thomas, or any two of them. And moreover, to cause proclamation to be made, in all those parts, for the perpetual observance of them , and likewise to do all other things for the safety and defence of the said marsh, in exclusion and evacuation of those waters, as should be necessary and proper. And lastly, to inquire by the oaths of honest and lawful men of that country, of all the confederacies and practices before mentioned , as also of such trespasses and contempts, as had been made against the said king, by the before-mentioned Matthew and his accomplices.

By virtue of which precept, the said Thomas, Robert, and Thomas, (a) being met at Crowethorne, on Monday next after the feast of the translation of St Thomas the martyr, in the year above-said ; by the consent of the lords of the towns, the bailiff, xxiv, jurors and commonalty of the said marsh , viz by John Francis, attorney to Simon, archbishop of Canterbury ; the abbot of St. Augustines in Canterbury ; the prior of Christ Church in Canterbury ; Simon, master of God's House in Dover ; Edmund Staplegate, lord of Nether Bilsyngton ; and other lords to this purpose specially elected, with certain likewise of the commonalty ; scil William de Echyngham, Stephen de Valeynes, &c chosen likewise for the said commonalty, did ordain and appoint, 1. that the common bailiff of the said marsh, (b) who had lands and residence therein, should be elected by the public consent of the lords of the towns of the said marsh, or their special attornies ; and where the greater number consented, the choice to stand . which election to be made at Demecherche or Newcherche, or some other fit place, within the compass of the said marsh, in the xvᵐᵉ of S. Michael, yearly, upon summons of the aforesaid bailiff · except upon necessity and reasonable cause, the said bailiff ought to be removed, within that year, and another chosen in his place.

2. If the person so elected, shall be present, and refuse to undergo the said office, that he
be

a Pat 35 E. III. p. 1. m. 6. in dorso.  b Adhuc ex præf. cod. MS. penes Will. le Neve Clar. Regem Armorum. an. 1940.

be forthwith amerced in xl*s*. to be levied by the succeeding bailiff, upon his goods and chattels, for the common benefit of the said marsh: and forthwith a new choice to be made of another bailiff, who will undergo that office, and take his oath, and receive for his fee the double of all the money assessed upon any person for such negligence. And if the person so neglected, shall be afterwards hindered by any man, so that he dare not undergo the office, that then the parties so hindering him, to be severally punished by the said electors, in such sort as the said bailiff should have been punished, if he had refused to take his oath, and to bear the same office

3 If it should happen so, that he who shall so be chosen, be absent at the time of election, all his goods and chattels to be forthwith distrained, by the preceding bailiff of the marsh, and impounded in proper and convenient places, and there detained until he shall repair to the archbishop of Canterbury, abbot of S. Augustines, and prior of Christ Church, for the time being, or to one of them, and accept of the said office, and take his oath, and thereupon carry to the preceding bailiff his letters sealed, and this he shall do within six days after the election made, and if he do not, then to be punished as aforesaid, and a new election to be presently made

4. At which principal Last, if the said common collectors of all the former general taxes will be present, they shall make their account to the bailiff, xxiv jurors, and commonalty of the said marsh, which account to be written by indentures, made between them and the bailiff, xxiv jurors and commonalty of the said marsh, and after the same manner shall the bailiff make his account of those things, which belong to him.

If any of the xxiv jurors shall make default in the said principal Last, except he may have a reasonable excuse, he shall be amerced in xiid. to be levied by the bailiff, to the use of the commonalty.

5 If it shall happen, that any of the xxiv jurors do depart within the year, or ought to be removed, that then another be made choice of in his place, and put in the said principal Last, by the lords of the fees, bailiff, xxiv jurors and commonalty, of the most faithful, discreet, and wealthy men of the said marsh, to the number of xxiv compleat.

6 In like manner it shall be done concerning the collectors and expenditors, so that they be not chosen out of the said xxiv jurors if the lords will be there. And if the said xxiv jurors, collectors or expenditors, shall be chosen, and will not take his oath, he shall be amerced in xxs. to be levied as aforesaid, and immediately another chosen in his place, and receive the charge.

7 If the before mentioned xxiv jurors shall be summoned within the precinct of the said marsh, to the common or several Last, where no more than eight or ten, at the most, do come; by which means there can be no judgement and decree made for the safety of the said Marsh, considering the absence of the greater number; that then every absent person shall be amerced by the bailiff in vid. to be levied as aforesaid; of which the said bailiff shall make account in the principal Last

8. Every one of the xxiv jurymen shall swear, that he will, together with his colleagues justly make all judgements and decrees, not favouring rich or poor, either in making distresses, or in whatever may concern the banks, land-eaus, water-gangs, sewers, and drains or the removing of bridges, and other impediments whatever, within the precinct of the said Marsh, and punishing trespassers, and that they be observant to the bailiff of the said marsh, for the valuing and selling of the distresses, taken and impounded for three days or more in the places accustomed; and that they cause all the judgements and decrees, by them made to be inrolled and an indenture to be made between them and the men of the said marsh, for the time being

9 Likewise the collectors and expenditors, chosen as aforesaid, shall swear, that they will faithfully levy, collect, disburse and make account of all the taxes and assessments, made by the lords, bailiff, and xxiv jurors, or the greater part of them; and the same course shall
be

be obferved in all the water-gangs within the precinct of the faid marfh, and before every of the lords of the towns, if they will be prefent.

10. Alfo the bailiff fhall fwear, that he will make faithful execution of the judgements and decrees of the before-mentioned xxiv jurors, and of thofe things which do belong to them, to judge and determine, as alfo, that in his proper perfon, he will charge upon all the collectors and expenditors, by oath, that they fhall faithfully levy, collect, difburfe, and account for, as well all general taxes, as feveral water-gangs fo affeffed, as aforefaid, and that he will, in perfon, take view of all the banks, land-eaus, water-gangs, fewers, drains, and bridges, when need fhall require, at leaft twice in the year, viz. once in the month of January, and afterwards in the month of June, and that he will deliver unto his fucceffor, all the evidences which he may have in his cuftody, as well the charters of the kings of England, concerning the liberties and cuftoms of the faid marfh, as the rolls of judgements, decrees and awards, made by the faid xxiv jurors, with every procefs of accounts of the collectors and expenditors, whatever, done in their times, and the clerk of the faid bailiff fhall have, for his fee, from the commonalty of the faid marfh, viz. viii *d.*

11. Moreover, it fhall not be lawful for any man, to make any dams or fords, or other impediment, in any land-eaus, water-gangs, drains, or common water-courfes, in the faid marfh, by which the right courfe of the waters may in any fort be impeded, and if they fhall fo do, and teftimony given thereof, by the bailiff and fix of the jurors, or the commonalty, of the watercourfe, where fuch damage fhall be made, he fhall be forthwith amerced, according to the proportion of his offence, by the faid bailiff and xxiv. jurors, which amercement to be likewife forthwith levied, to the common benefit, as aforefaid, and neverthelefs if any other than the commonalty fhall receive damage by that means, and that proof be made thereof, by the teftimony of the bailiff and fix jurors, fatisfaction fhall be made to him for the fame.

12. Likewife they did ordain and appoint,

that every tax affeffed in the faid marfh, fhould be proclaimed in certain public places, and a day of payment thereupon affigned: and this proclamation to be fo made, that no man might plead ignorance, as to the time and place he ought to pay it.

13. They did farther ordain and decree, that every acre, for the banks, in drains, and water-gangs, be bought for xls and that it fhall not be lawful for any man, to draw away any workmen, being in the public work, for his own private employment, nor to take them to any other place, till that work be perfected. and if any man fhall be found faulty by the teftimony of the bailiff, or jurors, in the common Laft, he fhall be amerced in xs to be forthwith levied by the faid bailiff, to the common benefit, as aforefaid.

14 Alfo they ordained and decreed, that all the water-courfes within the faid marfh, by whatever lands and tenements, in each channel be fo kept, that the water fhall not run out of its right courfe, to the damage of any man, upon penalty of the value thereof, to be levied by the faid bailiff, for the behalf of the commonalty, when any fhall be found guilty in the common Laft, by the teftimony of the bailiff and fix jurors

15. Becaufe, of antient time, it was appointed by the king, that all the maritime lands, from the ifle of Thanet, to Pevenefe, as well in the county of Kent, as county of Suffex, fhould be governed by the laws, ordinances, ftatutes, and cuftoms of the faid marfh of Romene, it fhall be lawful to the faid bailiff and xxiv jurors, to require and have his reafonable charges, of thofe who fhall have a mind to bring them to the places, be they lords, or of the commonalty, where they ought to make their ordinance, according to the maritime law, as well in the banks as water-gangs drains, fewers, and fifhings, and other things whatever relating to that law.

16. And laftly they ordained and decreed, that if any perfon fhould make a refcue from the bailiff of the marfh, or his officers, of any diftrefs whatever, taken by any of them, by virtue
of

of the before-mentioned articles, or any ordinance made, or to be made, for the benefit of the said marsh, and be found guilty by the testimony of the said bailiff, and six or eight of the said xxiv jurors; or of the water-course, where the distress shall happen to be taken, he shall be amerced in xls to be levied by the bailiff, for the use of the commonalty, as aforesaid And in the same manner it shall be done in those places, where the maritime law is used, within the isle of Thanet and Pevenese, whether in Kent, or Suffex.

After this, I have not met with any thing else, of this marsh, worthy observation, until 43° E. III. that the before-mentioned Thomas de Lodelowe, as also Robert Belknap, John Woodhall, Roger Dygge, William Topclive, and William Horne, were constituted commissioners for overseeing the banks and drains therein. (a) Nor from that time till 48 E III. that William Latymere, constable of Dover castle, and warden of the Cinque ports, Thomas Reynes, then his lieutenant, Roger Dygge, and some others, were assigned by the king, to view the banks, water-courses, &c. (b) thereof, lying betwixt the towns of Hethe and Newendon. By which commission they had power to impress so many carpenters and other labourers, as they should judge necessary for the accomplishment of the work in hand, wherever they could be found, within the county of Kent.

To king Edward the third succeeded Richard the second; in the first year of whose reign, it appears that Richard de Horne, Stephen Wettenham, John Franceys, and Hamon Wodeman, were put in commission, to supervise the banks in this marsh, (c) from the town of Hethe, along the sea-coast to Apuldre; as also in other marshes within this county, viz. from the haven of Romney, to Promhill church, and from thence by the sea-coast to Apuldre before-mentioned, they being at that time in decay, in many places. Which king (viz Richard the second) out of his special care also for the safety of this marsh, having viewed the charter of his royal ancestor king Edward the first; wherein as well that of king Henry the third, of which I have taken

notice in its proper place, as that memorable ordinance of Henry de Bathe, are recited; did not only confirm them both: but farther, out of his princely favour, by the assent of his council, at the request of the inhabitants of the said marsh, (a) granted for himself and his heirs, to the bailiff and xxiv jurors, which then were, and should be, that they, as also their heirs and successors, should for ever have this liberty, viz. they and every of them, to be exempt from serving at any assizes, on juries, inquisitions, or recognitions, as well within this county of Kent, as out of it, excepting in what should relate to the said king, or his heirs. And that neither they, nor any of them should be sheriff, escheator, bailiff, collector of tenths or fifteenths, or of any other subsidy, charge, tax, or tallage, to be granted to him the said king, or his heirs; or any other officer or minister to him or his heirs aforesaid, against their own good-will, during the time that they or any of them should be in the said office of bailiff, or one of the jury aforesaid. And the reason of this his royal grant, for such immunity, he there declares; viz. that by their absence, the whole marsh, as he had been informed, might be overflown in a very short time; and so, utterly lost and destroyed, to the great peril and damage of all his liege subjects in those parts

In like manner, and with the like recitals, at large, did king Henry the fourth, and king Henry the sixth, (b) confirm the said charter of king Henry the third, and the so-often-mentioned laws and ordinances of Henry de Bathe, concerning this marsh; adding the like liberties and privileges, as king Richard the second by his charter, last before observed, ordained.

Which said laws, with all the others relating to this marsh, as also the customs aforesaid, were grown at length so famous, that the said king Henry the sixth, (c) in the sixth year of his reign, by the advice and consent of the lords spiritual and temporal, and at the special instance of the commons of this realm, then assembled in parliament, holden at Westminster, having considered the great damage and losses, which had often been sustained by the excessive

rising

---

a Pat 43 E III. p m. 30 in dorso  b Pat 48 E III. p 1 m. 30. in dorso.  c Pat. 1 R. II. 1 m 25 in dorso.

a Pat 14 R. II p 2 m 38  b. Pat. 10 H IV p. 1. m 17.—Pat 8 H. VI. p. 1 m. 21.  c Inter Statuta de an. 6 H. VI. cap. 5.

rifing of waters in many parts of the realm; and that much greater was like to enfue, if remedy were not fpeedily provided: and thereupon ordaining and granting, that for ten years next enfuing, feveral commiffions of fewers fhould be made to feveral perfons by the chancellor of England, for the time to come, in all parts of this his realm, where it fhould be needful, the form of which commiffion is there recited, amongft other things gave to the faid commiffioners fpecial power and direction, by that act, " to make and ordain proper ftatutes and or- " dinances, for the fupport and prefervation of " the fea-banks and marfhes, and the parts ad- " jacent, according to the laws and cuftoms of " this Romney Marfh "

And after the expiration of the faid ten years, by act of parliament in 18 of his reign, (a) continued the fame form of commiffions. So likewife in 23, the like did king Edward the fourth in 12° of his reign; and king Henry the feventh in 4° of his.

And now having thus fhewn how great a care and regard the fucceffive kings of this realm had, for feveral ages, of this famous marfh, I will clofe up what I have farther to fay, with that memorable charter of king Edward the fourth, bearing date at Weftminfter 23° February, in the firft year of his reign, by which he incorporated the bailiff, and jurors thereof, the tenor of which is as follows; viz. That whereas he the faid king, held himfelf obliged to take care of the defence of this his realm, and his loyal fubjects, from what place foever, efpecially thofe who lay neareft to the firft affaults, and attempts of his enemies. And confidering, that many towns and places, fituate near the fea, had been laid wafte by the fpoils and burnings of the faid enemies. and through the terrors of the inhabitants, who fometime had deferted them, left uninhabitable and defolate: thinking it therefore moft neceffary, to repair the faid towns and places, or to new-build others near them; and being fo built, to endow and confirm them with liberties and privileges, that being fo fortified, they may, by the people's recourfe to them, be made more powerful and

ftrong, for the better fafety of the whole country. And confidering that in this marfh of Romeney in the county of Kent, which is fituate near the fea, there was not at that time fuch a refort of people and inhabitants, as were ufed to be: but were it better defended, there would be a much greater confluence thereto, for the greater fafety of the whole country, as he the faid king had been informed from the credible relation of the inhabitants of the faid marfh, and other parts adjacent.

Taking therefore the premifes into confideration, of his fpecial grace and favour, at the inftant requeft of all the commonalty and inhabitants in the faid marfh, as alfo for the prefervation thereof, and greater fecurity of the adjacent towns, he gave and granted to the faid inhabitants, refiding in the limits and bounds thereof, that they fhould be one body in fubftance and name, and one commonalty perpetually incorporate of one bailiff and xxiv jurors, and the commonalty of the faid Romeney marfh in the county of Kent, for ever. That the faid bailiff, jurors, and commonalty fhall have a continual fucceffion, and they and their fucceffors for ever called, termed and named by the name of the bailiff, jurors and commonalty of Romeney marfh in the county of Kent. That they and their fucceffors fhall be perfons proper and capable in law to purchafe lands and tenements, and other poffeffions whatever, to themfelves and their fucceffors, to enjoy in fee and perpetuity. That they fhall have a common feal for their affairs and bufineffes, relating to them the faid bailiff, jurors, and commonalty, and their fucceffors and fhall plead and be impleaded, anfwer and be anfwered, by the name of the bailiff, jurors and commonalty of Romeney marfh, in the county of Kent, in every of the faid king's courts, and the courts of his heirs and fucceffors, and in all other courts and places whatever. Which faid bailiff and jurors, to be elected in like manner and form; as alfo exercife their offices, and be difplaced from them, as formerly was accuftomed in the faid marfh.

Moreover, that the faid bailiff, jurors and commonalty, and their fucceffors fhall have a
certain

a 18 H. VI. cap. 10.—23 H VI. c 9 —12 E. IV. c. 6 —4 H. VII c. 1.

Marquis Townshend

# DRAINING:

The *Cheapeſt WORK ever offered to the Public, and will be publiſhed on* TUESDAY *the Firſt Day of* MAY, 1792, *and continued.*

## Number I,

(PRICE, ONLY TWO SHILLINGS,)
O F

# DUGDALE's HISTORY
OF
## IMBANKING AND DRAINING
T H E
## FENS AND MARSHES,
Both in FOREIGN PARTS, and in this KINGDOM:
And of the Improvements intended thereby;

EXTRACTED FROM
## RECORDS, MANUSCRIPTS, AND OTHER AUTHENTIC TESTIMONIES:
Reviſed, and Corrected from the EDITION of 1662,
WITH SEVERAL NEW ADDITIONS.

By the REVEREND GEORGE WILLIAM LEMON,
Rector of *Geyton Thorpe*, and Vicar of *Eaſt Walton.*

LYNN. Printed and Sold by W WHITTINGHAM; and may be had of S. CROWDER, Paternoſter-Row, *London*, HODSON and LUNN, *Cambridge*, YARRINGTON and BACON, *Norwich*; JACOB, *Peterborough*, PEAT and NEWCOMB, *Stamford*; DRUMMOND, *Lincoln*; JENKINSON, *Huntingdon*; CROFTS, *Saint Ives*, RUFFHEAD, *Bedford*; GOULD, *Spalding*; Mr GENN, the Lamb Inn, *Ely*; CORDRAN, *Yarmouth*; PRESTON, *Boſton*, and THOROUGOOD, *Downham.*

### TO THE PUBLIC.

THIS firſt Number will be embelliſhed with an elegant Engraved Plate, of the late Mr. KINDERLEY's various intended Cuts for the better Draining the Fen Lands, bordering on the River Ouze.

And the remaining eight Numbers to contain one, or two Copper Plates, new and elegantly engraved in a ſuperior manner to what they are in Dugdale's laſt Edition, publiſhed by Charles Nalſon Cole, Eſq

They will be printed according to the Specimen, with a good Type, and fine Paper, making One Large Volume Quarto

Great Pains and Expence have been employed in rendering this WORK, worthy the approbation of the Public and after the Publication of theſe Numbers, it will not be ſold under a Guinea and a Half

Lately publiſhed from the ſame Preſs,—The REPORT of Meſſrs. GOLBORNE, and MYLNE, on the propoſed NEW CUT.

Likewiſe in the Preſs, and ſpeedily will be publiſhed,—The Hiſtory of the CIVIL WARS, between YORK and LANCASTER, by the Rev. Mr. LEMON.

DEDICATED TO HIS GRACE THE
## *DUKE OF BEDFORD.*

# PROPOSALS,

For PRINTING by SUBSCRIPTION,

*From an Original Manuscript;*

AN HISTORICAL ACCOUNT OF THE

## *Great Level of the Fens, call'd*

# BEDFORD LEVEL,

And other FENS, MARSHES, and Low-Lands in this
Kingdom and other Places:

With References to LELAND's *Itinerary,* DUGDALE's *History of
Imbanking and Draining,* and others of the moſt approved Authority:

In which will be deſcribed the antient natural ſtate of the ſaid Great Level, and the rivers paſſing
through it, the changes and alterations they have undergone, the great and expenſive works which
have been erected for the improvement of it, with the ſucceſs and miſcarriages attending them,
affording uſeful and inſtructive examples in future undertakings of the like nature.

By WILLIAM ELSTOBB, late *Land-Surveyor and Engineer.*

### C O N D I T I O N S.

I. That this work will be neatly printed in
one volume octavo, with a good type and fine
paper

II The price to ſubſcribers, 12s. for the *large
paper,* and 7s 6d. for the ſmall, to be paid on

delivery of the book in boards

III. Sir JONAS MOORE's reduced Map of the
great Level of the Fens ſhewing the plan of Mr
KINDERLEY's intended New Cuts, with a large
Map of *Marſhland. &c*

SUBSCRIPTIONS, taken in by W, WHITTINGHAM, Printer, LYNN, and all other Bookſellers.

### A LIST OF SUBSCRIBERS.

ASHLEY, Mr. Philip *Spalding,* l. p.
Andrews, Mr. Thomas *Walpole. do.*
Aſhley, Rev Mr. *Fleet,* l. p.
Aveling, Mr. Thomas *Whittleſea,* l. p.
Aveling, Mr. James *Whittleſea,*
Allen, Mr. W. Printer, *Grantham,*
Andrews, Mr. G *Elm,* l. p.
Brownlow, Rt. Hon Lord 2 copies, l p.
Banks, Sir Joſeph Bart l. p.
Bunbury, Sir T. C. Bart. 2 copies, l. p.
Buckworth, Rev. LL. D. l. p.
Bell, Henry Eſq *Lynn,* l. p
Bagge, William Eſq *Lynn,* l. p.
Bagge, Thomas Eſq. *Lynn,* l. p.
Beridge, Rev. Mr *Baſil,* l. p.
Bentham, Rev Mr. *Ely.*
Braithwaite, Rev Mr *Terrington,* l. p.
Bentinck, W. Eſq l. p.
Buckworth, Theop Eſq *Spalding,* l. p.
Birkbeck, Mr. J. Banker, *Lynn,* l. p.

Bellamy, Mr. J. Attorney, *Wiſbech,* l p.
Bowker, Mr. J. *Lynn.*
Brown, Mr. S. *Peterborough,* l. p.
Batterham, Mr Jos *Wiſbech*
Burton, Mr. Page *Upwell.* l. p.
Bagge, Mr F. *Ely.*
Brackenbury, Mr M *Ely.*
Baker, Mr. J. *Upwell.*
Booth, Mr. R. *Huntingdon.*
Brewerton, Mr Thomas *Walton,*
Bailey, Mr. John *Thorney,*
Barber, Mr James *Do.*
Bailey, Mr. Charles *Lynn,* l. p
Bean, Mr. *Walton*
Bellamy, Mr. Thomas *Standground,*
Boyce, Mr. John *Ely,* l. p.
Burnham, Mr. Bookſ. *Northamp.* 3 cop.
Brighton, Mr. T Attor. *Downham,* l.p.
Bedford Level, Hon. Corp. of, 6 co. l.p.
Barley, Mr. Attorney, *March.*

# SUBSCRIBERS.

Conway, Hon. Hugh Seymour, l. p.
Cooper, William Esq. 2 copies, l. p.
Coke, T. W. Esq. *Holkham*, 6 cop .l. p.
Cartwright, J. Esq. *Marnham, Nottingh.*
Cole, Henry Esq. *Peterborough*, l. p.
Cony, R. Esq. *Walpole*, l. p.
Cary, John Esq, *Lynn*, l. p.
Cole, Rev. Mr. *Ely.*
Case, Thomas Esq. *Testerdon*, l. p.
Coates, Mr. Dan. *Tilney*, l. p.
Cross, Mr. E. *Leverington* l. p.
Chapman, Mr. T. *Elm*. l. p.
Custance, Mr G *Upwell*. l. p.
Clay, R. Esq *Whitechurch, Salop*. l. p.
Clay, C. Esq. *Ditto*
Crisp, Mr. J *Lynn.*
Creasy, Mr. John *Fordham*, 1 p.
Clark. Mr W Attorney *Wisbech.*
Dean and Chapter, (The) of *Ely.*
Cole Charl. Nalson, Esq Fen-Office, l.p.
Creasy, Mr. W. *Downham*, in the *Isle*, l. p.
Case, Philip, Esq *Lynn*, l. p.
Dashwood, F P Esq *Well Valley.*
Donken, Mr R. *Wisbech.*
Dunn, Mr W. *Chatteris.*
Dugmore, Mr *Swaffham*. l p.
Dow, Mr. William *Elm*, l p.
Dow, Mr John, *Do.* l. p.
Dering, J T. Esq *Crow-hall*, l p.
Evans, Mr. H. R. *Ely*, l. p.
Edes, J Esq; *Wisbech*, l p.
Edwards, Mr John *Soham.*
Ewen, Mr T. G *Norwich*, l. p.
Fyre, Mr. John *Feltwell*, l. p
Edmonds, Mr Surveyor *Peterboro'* l p.
Folkes, Sir M. B. Bart l. p.
Fountaine, Brigg Esq. *Narford*, l. p.
Frusher, Mr. W. *Elm*, l p.
Jydell, Thomas Esq *Boston*, l. p.
Fawlett, Mr. T. Attorney, *Wisbech*, l p
Fydell, Mr. T *Lynn*,
Failes, Mr James *Upwell*,
Freeman, Mr. J. *Sutton in the Isle*, l. p,
Grimditch, R. Esq *Chatteris.*
Goodman, Mr. N. *March.*
Grounds, Mr. H *Ditto.*
Gibbons, Mr. J *Lutton* l p
Golborne, Mr J. Engineer, *Ely.* l p
Girdlestone, Rev. Mr. J. *Thorney*, l. p.
Green, Mr. C. M. Attorney *Spalding*,
Ground, Mr Edward *Whittlesea*, l. p.
Ground, Mr. W. D. *Do.* 3 copies l p.
Gray, Mr. Owen *March*, l. p
Garland, Mr. W Long Sutton.
Gillam, Mr. J. Merchant, *Cambridge*, l.p.

Hardwick, Rt. Hon. the Earl of l. p.
Harvey, Mr. W. *Clement's Inn, London*, l.p.
Hutcheson, Mr. M. *Wisbech.*
Haynes, Mr. H. Merch. *Whittlesea*, l. p.
Hovell, Mr. *Downham.* l p
Holman, Mr. T. *Downham*, l. p.
Hawkes, Mr. T. *Spalding.*
Howell, Mr. Joseph *Elm*, l. p.
Hart, Capt. G. *Peterborough*,
Herbert, Mr. D. *Biggleswade*, l p
Holland, Mr. H. *Moulton*,
Houchen, Mr. John *Wereham*. l. p.
Hare, Mr. Castor
Hancock, Mr. E. *Fulham, Camb.* l. p.
Hemington, Mr. J Attorney *Lynn*, l. p.
Hodgkinson, J. Esq; Engineer, *Lond.* l.p.
Jenyns, the Rev. Mr. l. p.
Johnson, Rev. Mr. M. *Spalding*, l. p.
Johnson, Mr. G. *Leverington*, l. p.
Johnson, Mr. J. *Leverington*, l. p.
Johnson, Fairfax Esq. *Spalding*, l. p.
Johnson, Mr. John *Whittlesea*, l. p.
Johnson, Mr. Thomas *Do.* l. p.
Johnson, Mr. H March, l p.
Jacob, Mr. J. *Peterborough*,
Jessop, W. Esq. Engineer, *Newark*, l. p.
Jones, Mr. M. *London*, l p.
Lunn, Mr, Bookseller, *Cambridge*, 6 l.
   and 3 small.
Lemon, the Rev Mr. G.W. *Walton*, l. p.
King, Wm. Esq. near *Lincoln*, l. p.
Kenrick, Mr. *Whitechurch, Salop.*
Key, Mr. J. sen. *Holbech*, l. p.
Key, Mr. J. jun. *Ditto*,
Kelk, J. Esq. *Postland*, l. p.
Lindsay, Hon. and Rev. Mr. *Wisbech*, l.p.
Lumpkin, Mr. N. *Leverington.* l p
Lee, Mr. J. *Upwell*, l p.
Lee, Mr. J. *Lynn.*
Lee, Mr. W. *Upwell*, l. p.
Laughton, Mr. Charles *Wisbech*,
Long, Mr. James *Upwell*, l p
Lewin, Mr. R. H *March*, l. p.
Miles, Jeaffreson Mr. *Fakenham*, l. p.
Mayer, Mr. J. Attorny, *Wisbech*, l p
Moore, Rev. Mr. Thomas *Peterb* l. p.
Maydwell, Mr. Henry *Whittlesea*, l. p.
Moss, Mr. T. sen. *March*, l p
Marshall, Mr J. *Elm*, l. p
Matland, Mr. C. *Lynn*, l. p.
Maxwell, —— Esq. *Fletton*, l. p.
Micklefield, Mr. R. *Stoke*,
Mylne, R. Esq. Engineer, *London*, l p
Mann, Mr. J. *Tilney* l p
Martin, Mr. J. *Outwell*, l. p.

Martin, Mr. Matthew *Newton*,
Martin, Mr. W. *Downham in the Isle*, l. p.
Marshall, Mr. J. *Upwell*,
Northon, Mayor *Holbech*, l. p.
Noble, F. Esq. *Ely*, l. p.
Orford, The Rt. Hon the Earl 6 cop. l p
Peyton, Lady *Hagbeck-Hall*, l. p.
Portland, His Grace the Duke of 6 cop.
Plestow, T. B. Esq. *Watlington*, l. p.
Pemberton, Rev. Mr. A. M. *Upwell*, l p
Peckard, Rev. Dr. *Fletton*,
Pery, Rev. Mr. Wyten *Huntingdon*.
Parke, Rev. Mr. G W *St·German's*. l. p
Pearson, Rev. Mr. J. *Upwell*. l. p.
Peart, Joshua Esq. *L. Sutton*, 2 cop. l. p.
Pratt, E. R. Esq. Ruston Hall l. p.
Peckover, Mr. J. *Wisbech*.
Pigot, Mr. R. *Ely*, l. p.
Powell, Mr William *Wisbech*, l. p.
Partridge, Henry Esq, l. p.
Pate, Mr. Robert *Thorney*.
Plummer, Mr. George *Whittlesea*,
Poulter, Mr. *Upwell*, l. p.
Payne, Mr. *Chatteris*,
Peary, Mr. James
Page, Mr. T. *Ely*, l. p.
Page, Mr. Thomas jun. *Ely*, l. p.
Pechey, J. Esq. *Soham*, l. p.
Pearson, Mr. R. Attorney, *Soham*, l. p
Rennie, J. Esq; Engineer, Surry-street,
 Black-Friars, *London*, l. p.
Rayner, Mr. William *Wisbeach*, l. p.
Ripshaw, Mr. Joseph *Ditto*, l. p.
Rowley, O Esq, *Huntingdon*, l.p.
Stafford, Rt Hon. Marquis of 6 *cop.l.p.*
Squire, Mr. Thomas *Peterborough*, l p.
Squire, Mr. William *Do·*
Stokes, Mr. W *Fakenham*, l p.
Swaine, Mr. Spilman *Leverington*, l p.
Smart, Mr. R. *Welney*, l. p.
Scott, Mr. G. *Ditto*, l. p.
Spooner, Mr. N. *Ely*, l. p.
Sutton, Mr. R. *Upwell*, l. p.
Saffery, Mr E. *Downham*. l. p.

Skrimshire, Mr. William, *Wisbech*, l. p.
Sutton, Mr. Joseph *Thorney*,
Smith, Mr William *Do.* l. p.
Still, Mr Edward *Do.*
Stanger, Mr. Jos. *Tidd, St·Mary's*,
Sudbury, Mr. John *Whittlesea*, l. p.
Simkin, Mr. Thomas *Peterborough*.
Sanderson, Mr. Attorney, *Spalding*, l. p.
Stevens, Mr. Samuel *Wisbech*, l. p.
Savory, Mr. C. *Syderstone*, l. p.
Self, Mr. L. Merchant, Lynn, l. p.
Swansborough, Mr. John *Wisbech*.
Smith, Mr. Sim. *Whittlesea*, l. p.
Trafford, Lady *Wisbech*, l. p.
Trollope, Sir John Bart. l. p.
Townshend, Mr. W. *Downham*, l. p.
Thacker, Mr. Ant. *Upwell*, l. p.
Tansley, Mr. Henry *Little-Port*, l. p.
Tansley, Mr Henry jun. *Ditto*, l. p.
Townley, R. G. Esq. l. p.
Underwood, Rev. Mr Preb. of *Ely*, l p.
Venn, Rev. Mr. J. *Dunham*.
Vitty, Mr. R. *Ely*, l p.
Wodehouse, Sir J. B. *Kimberly*, 6 cop l p
Warner, H. Lee Esq. 20 *copies*, l. p.
Wing, J. Esq. *Thorney*, l p.
Wool, Mr. H. *Upwell*, l p.
Wood, Mr J *Walpole*.
Watts, Mr T. *Lynn*.
Wainman, Oglethorpe M D. 2 cop. l. p.
Watson, Mr. Thomas *Thorney*, l. p.
Walker, Mr. J. *Sutton*, l p.
Wallis, Mr. W. *Do.* l p.
Walcot, Mr. *Oundle*,
Watts, Mr. J. Engineer, *Wisbech*, l. p.
Watford, Mr. Thomas *Upwell*,
Waudby, Mr. W *March*, l p.
Wright, Mr T *Upwell*, l p
Wilkin, Mr. W. Attorney, *Soham*, l. p.
Wild, Mr R. St. John's, *Soham*.
Wallis, Mr. R. *Hauxton* near *Cambridge*.
Yorke, C. Esq. Lord Judge of the *Isle of*
 *Ely*, l p.
Young, Mr. Rich. *Walton*, l p.

N. B. *The* EDITOR *is much obliged to the Reverend Gentleman of* BURY, *and the Gentleman at* SPALDING, *for the Additions they have been pleased to communicate: and any Nobleman, or Gentleman, who may be in possession of any manuscript, or work, relating to* DUGDALE, *and will be pleased to communicate it to the Editor, it shall be inserted; and the book or manuscript, carefully returned, with all due acknowlegement.*

Lightning Source UK Ltd.
Milton Keynes UK
UKOW05f1029030516

273458UK00001B/203/P